Cosmopolitan Lives on the Cusp of Empire

Jane Haggis • Clare Midgley • Margaret Allen • Fiona Paisley

Cosmopolitan Lives on the Cusp of Empire

Interfaith, Cross-Cultural and Transnational Networks, 1860–1950

palgrave
macmillan

Jane Haggis
College of Humanities, Arts and Social Science
Flinders University
Adelaide, South Australia, Australia

Margaret Allen
Gender Studies and Social Analysis
University of Adelaide
Adelaide, South Australia, Australia

Clare Midgley
Department of Humanities
Sheffield Hallam University
Sheffield, United Kingdom

Fiona Paisley
School of Humanities, Languages, and Social Science
Griffith University
Brisbane, Queensland, Australia

ISBN 978-3-319-52747-5 ISBN 978-3-319-52748-2 (eBook)
DOI 10.1007/978-3-319-52748-2

Library of Congress Control Number: 2017937903

Cover image: Pattern adapted from an Indian cotton print produced in the 19th century

Printed on acid-free paper

This Palgrave Macmillan imprint is published by Springer Nature
The registered company is Springer International Publishing AG
The registered company address is: Gewerbestrasse 11, 6330 Cham, Switzerland

Preface

The idea for this book and our collaboration coalesced through conversation at conferences and other gatherings where we shared bits and pieces of evidence about our various research into matters of religion, empire, gender and race. We became increasingly aware of synergies and connections between our different research data sets. We began to discern how the vocabularies of colonial racial hierarchies appeared to be shifting around through articulations of faith and affect that did not conform to the binaries of empire taken for granted in much of the New Imperial History. An uneven, ambiguous and at times, contradictory, opening up of new imaginaries of interfaith and cross-cultural universalisms seemed discernible in quite unexpected spaces, places and networks. It was this that inspired us to collaborate in writing this volume: that a story about liberal religion and cosmopolitanism was an important and thus far, largely untold dimension of the cosmopolitanisms and internationalisms that presaged the end of empire and the framing of global community shaped in the post-world war emphasis on universal rights and protections, however fractured with colonial legacies and new vectors of imperial power they proved to be.

Our collaboration has been a fruitful one for all involved. In spite, or because, of the global logistics involved in working together, whenever we did manage to gather in one place, the conversations were unusually rich and stimulating. In particular, a Flinders University Visiting International Research Fellowship awarded to Professor Melanie Oppenheimer and Jane Haggis allowed Clare Midgley to spend 3 weeks at Flinders University, Adelaide, and also brought Fiona Paisley to Flinders. The series of meetings held during this period were invaluable in shaping the form and content of this book. We were able to synthesise a conceptual framework of multiple cosmopolitanisms that gave a coherent framework to each of our historical case studies. In this way, we could drive our own work to engage with our intellectual synthesis: Clare Midgley wrote Chapter 2; Margaret Allen, Chapter 3; Jane Haggis, Chapter 4; and Fiona Paisley, Chapter 5. One of the most rewarding aspects of this structure was that we each read and re-read and commented on each other's chapters multiple times, as well as co-authoring in various ways Chapters 1 and 6. We believe this gives the book a tight conceptual framework while capturing the energy of our passion for our own research subjects to enliven the text and increase its accessibility. We hope our readers agree.

Any writing project involves more than just writing or even collaborating between the co-authors. The support of Professor Melanie Oppenheimer, then Dean of the School of History and International Relations at Flinders University, Adelaide, South Australia, and the Visiting Research Scholarship have been crucial. The preparation of this book has also been enabled by funding from the Faculty and School Research Grant Schemes at Flinders. The award of an Australian Research Council Discovery Project Grant (2017–2019) also assisted the completion of this book and the continuation of research into the themes raised in this volume. Jane Haggis wants to acknowledge the professionalism and generosity of her fellow authors who made the task of coordination so straightforward and who so generously shared their knowledge and insights to make this book what it is. Jane would also like to thank Callum Gare for his thoughtful conversations and careful technical and research assistance, as well as appropriately timed sweets and hot chai. Clare Midgley takes this opportunity to thank the staff of Women's Library at the London School of Economics for their friendly and generous assistance. Margaret Allen acknowledges Professor Uma Dhupelia-Mesthrie, University of the Western Cape, for sharing resources, including the photograph of Henry Polak; and the helpful staff at the Barr Smith Library, University of Adelaide. Fiona Paisley thanks Roshan DeSilva Wijeyeratne for the many discussions, and Sophie Loy-Wilson and Marilyn Lake for convening the 'Thinking Labour Rights through the "Coolie Question" Workshop' in September 2015 as part of the Laureate Research Program in International History and Race and Ethnicity in the Global South at the University of Sydney. Their workshop encouraged her to think about Indian labour conditions in the context of Pan-Pacific internationalism. Clare, Fiona and Margaret would particularly like to thank Jane for her pivotal role in pushing forward this project, and bringing the final manuscript together.

Contents

List of Figures

CHAPTER 1

Friendship, Faith and Cosmopolitan Thought Zones on the Cusp of Empire

Abstract The legacies of colonialism continue to resonate, in a new era of intensified globalisation that once again places race and religion at the centre of a search for peaceful co-existence. This book looks back to the period 1860–1950 in order to grasp how alternative visions of amity and co-existence were forged between people of faith, within but resistant to imperial contact zones. This chapter contextualises our argument that networks of faith and friendship played a vital role in forging new vocabularies of cosmopolitanism that presaged the post-imperial world of the 1950s.

Keywords Cosmopolitanism · Race · Provincialise Europe · Affect · Religion · India · Christianity

In 1903 W. E. B. Du Bois, the eminent African American sociologist, wrote: 'The problem of the twentieth century is the problem of the colour line.'[1] His words are echoed by V. S. Azariah, an Indian Christian representative, speaking at the 1910 World Missionary Conference to a largely European audience: 'The problem of race relationships is one of the most serious problems confronting the Church today.'[2] The legacies of colonialism continue to resonate, in a new era of intensified globalisation that once again places race and religion at the centre of a search for peaceful co-existence, captured by the sociologist Stuart Hall's prescient observation

J. Haggis et al., *Cosmopolitan Lives on the Cusp of Empire*,
DOI 10.1007/978-3-319-52748-2_1

that 'the coming question of the twenty-first century' is how to fashion 'the capacity to live with difference'.[3] This book looks back to the period 1860–1950 in order to grasp how alternative visions of amity and co-existence were forged between people of faith, within but resistant to imperial contact zones. We argue that networks of faith and friendship played a vital role in forging new vocabularies of cosmopolitanism that presaged the post-imperial world of the 1950s, as demonstrated in the case studies discussed in the chapters that follow.

Rethinking Colonialism and Cosmopolitanism in Transnational and International History

The project of globalising imperial history has brought to the fore the multiple trajectories of 'coming together' between subjects otherwise on opposite sides of the global colour line. Over the past two decades, new histories of the intellectual and political impact of the vast movement of colonial and colonised subjects has reconfigured empire as dynamic sites articulated through intricate webs of connection, across and between binaries of power.[4]

Attention to non-Eurocentric and comparative cosmopolitanisms is a very recent historiographical trend. A number of recent studies[5] reveal that long before European hegemony, circuits of mobility produced expressions of cosmopolitanism in registers other than the body of thought shaped by a specific European intellectual history. Sugata Bose and Kris Manjapra[6] take this awareness a step further, pluralising cosmopolitanism and setting the concept adrift from its presumed European moorings. In so doing, they dismantle the binary relationship between coloniser and colonised as the singular bond within which anti- and post-imperial imaginaries were created. As they state, 'To frame the global circulation of ideas within the lone axis of centre versus periphery is to view the world through the colonial state's eyes and through its archive.'[7] Instead, a broader canvas is captured, one which is not limited, defined or derivative of European imperialisms' assumptions of universality or of European intellectual lineages of secular cosmopolitanism as arbiters of the modern.

Rather than rehearsing a progressive narrative from empire to post-empire, what emerges in the process is a dynamic and uneven terrain of contestation in a variety of locales concerning the legitimacy and future of imperial rule. Mrinalini Sinha, in her study of the 1930s controversy over the book *Mother India*, convincingly demonstrates how colonial events are inadequately captured in the interpretive framework of nationalist, anti-colonial versus imperial.[8] Even in the imperial metropolis of London in 1900, at the zenith of the empire, Schneer's study reveals how imperialist and anti-imperialist ideas jostled with each other for the attention of an increasingly multicultural population.[9] Satadru Sen's discussion of Kumar Shri Ranjitsinhji (1872–1933), an Indian representative to the League of Nations, draws out how these are expressed in the life of one individual who, through the migrancy of empire, exists in a 'liminal space between Empire and nation':

> His protestations of loyalty to the Empire and his simultaneous declarations of sympathy for anti-colonial positions might be seen as attempts to outline the contingencies of imperial cosmopolitanism: that is, the articulation of conditions under which an Indian who was also British might participate in Empire, nation, and colony, and in the wider world of empires, nations, and colonies.[10]

Nico Slate's *Colored Cosmopolitanism* reveals the solidarity forged across national and imperial borders between African American and Indian activists in a shared struggle for freedom, a hidden history of global solidarity that endured for almost a century.[11] More recently, Banivanua Mar[12] deconstructs how decolonisation in the Pacific is a long drawn-out and often hidden or denied history of indigenous globalisation that continues today. A history of 'displacement and dispossession' that has produced 'a unique, diasporic and stateless process of daily decolonisation characterised by a global connectivity'.[13]

This scholarship forms part of a larger endeavour to build a non-Eurocentric historiography of imperialism and modernity and to thus 'provincialise' European history.[14] We draw inspiration from this body of scholarship, which emphasises the problematic yet highly productive nature of various cosmopolitan visions that circulated and informed trans-colonial and transnational intellectual and political spaces, in ways that undermine the rendering of 'empire' or 'nation' into binaries such as coloniser/colonised or centre/periphery. It also challenges the depiction of this period as simply marked by a progressive trajectory from racialism to humanism.

In this book, we also consider how the tropes of emotion or feeling and affect as 'forces of encounter',[15] combine with faith (itself perhaps an emotion) to facilitate the coming together of people in new collective visions. Leela Gandhi, in her seminal study of the politics of friendship between metropolitan and anti-colonial radicalisms, writes of '"friendship" as the lost trope in anti-colonial thought'.[16] The chapters each develop this thread as it is prefigured in our earlier work on the affective dimensions of empire and imperialism. Friendship was also a primary trope in imperial Christianity, especially in the writings of the Protestant missionary movement. As Haggis and Allen argue for the period 1880–1920, 'friendship' operated in the writings of women missionaries in ambiguous and complex ways to connote a range of connections rather than a singular notion of friend.[17] Clare Midgley's ongoing research into liberal religion and the 'woman question' in the nineteenth-century world[18] focuses on a transnational network of 'kindred spirits' linking members of the Brahmo Samaj – an influential social and religious reform movement among Hindus – with British and American Unitarians, heterodox Protestants who were leading figures in social reform and in the early feminist movement. Her study reveals the multiple flows of influence, persuasion and affect circulating within this multinational network. As Fiona Paisley[19] argues for the Pan Pacific Women's Association, in transnational social justice movements cultural difference and race politics are routinely combined with a shared commitment to liberal Christian reformism in order to provide an affective basis for interpersonal and intellectual exchange.

It is a contention of this volume, following Manjapra,[20] that it was not only pre- and post-colonial contexts that were generative of 'other' cosmopolitanisms, but that the vortex of empire itself was also fertile ground for different cosmopolitanisms to emerge among middle-class, liberal and Christian subjects. Our volume takes forward this idea of the spaces of empire as being productive of ways of thinking and being cosmopolitan that are not straightforwardly derivative of Europe.

India and the Imperial World

India is the glue holding our case studies together, although geographically the chapters range across the British Empire, from Australia to London and beyond, to the USA and Japan. This reflects India's importance as one of the earliest, most important and most populous of British possessions: the 'Jewel in the Crown' in what was in the nineteenth and early twentieth centuries the most extensive and powerful European empire. By the start of our period in the 1860s, India had just been brought under crown rule following the violent suppression of the Great Rebellion of 1857. India lay at the centre of a complex 'contact zone' that, thanks to the very practices of colonial governance and political economy, spread to Fiji, the Caribbean, South Africa, Australia and Britain itself. India inspired the imperial imaginations of missionary societies, trading companies, officialdom and intellectuals, not only in terms of wealth, power and souls but as a civilisational entity whose culture appeared radically different from the norms of European civility. By 1950, the Indian subcontinent had gained its independence from Britain following an extended nationalist struggle which involved the forging of a range of new transnational connections extending beyond the borders of the empire.

The large Indian diaspora, initiated by pre-colonial trading relationships with the East coast of Africa, spread widely by means of the indentured labour system, initiated by the British in 1834 in order to provide servile and economical labour to plantations, largely within in British colonies.[21] The growing demands of expatriate Indians for better if not equal rights in the colonies to which they had been transported, and for an end to the system of indenture, created global networks, from Fiji and India to South Africa and the Caribbean. Leading members of the Indian nationalist movement were involved in these campaigns. Indeed, Mohandas Gandhi (1869–1948) built his early political career and ideas about Satyagraha or non-violent resistance, through participation in these campaigns as a young lawyer in South Africa during the period 1893–1914.

By 1860, colonial Indians were also deeply enmeshed in re-imagining themselves across the many fault-lines of contact. A new political community or nation was beginning to be articulated in anti-colonial nationalism by social groups who were themselves produced out of the interstices of colonial rule and imperial economy. A deep sense of the ancient lineage of Indian civilisation made 'tradition' and 'reform' the centrifuge through which Indian colonial society struggled against imperial rule and racism, and for a new sense of Indian modernity.[22] The Indian National Congress (INC), founded in 1885, took the lead in driving anti-colonial struggles to achieve independence, by 1906 adopting self-rule as its goal, achieved if necessary by direct action. This political strategy was fuelled by British recalcitrance, repression and even violence in the face of nationalist demands and political action.

Throughout this struggle for independence, Indian nationalists forged alliances and friendships internationally, not only with other colonised or racially oppressed peoples such as African Americans, but also with

Europeans who supported their cause, including British women and men. The contact zone of imperial missions was perhaps surprising ground for what Leela Gandhi insightfully refers to as 'affective communities of anti-colonial thought' but as Chapter 4 in this volume discusses, such communities could be enduring and effective.[23]

'India' exerted a powerful influence on the Western imagination, intellectually through the work of orientalist scholarship and in popular culture through the exoticisation of Indian bodies, practices and beliefs. On the one hand, a strict East versus West binary was constructed that, on the other, invited a romantic pre-occupation with bringing spiritual harmony through melding this binary. Earlier in the nineteenth century, transcendentalism was, perhaps, the first popularisation of 'Eastern religion' as a fruitful source of spiritual ideas to offset the hyper-materialism industrialisation seemed to demand. Theosophy was one of the more influential outgrowths of this search for meaning similarly drawing on 'Eastern spirituality' to proselytise universal spiritual truths that would harmonise 'east' with 'west'. It is no coincidence that both Transcendentalism and Theosophy appear in several of the case studies in this book. Less well explored are the ways in which imperial Christianity engaged with, and was re-shaped by, these counter-vocabularies of faith, identity and nation. Indeed, as the case studies in this volume demonstrate, faith and spirituality, including Christianity, were core components of new cosmopolitan thought zones in this period. Drawing on recent discussions of non-Western cosmopolitanisms, we discuss how new forms of cosmopolitanisms were generated within and between secular and religious encounters.[24]

From the late eighteenth century, British missionaries sought to convert Indians to Christianity, harnessing their evangelical zeal to imperialism under the protection of British colonial rule.[25] They were resoundingly unsuccessful in this ambition, with the number of conversions in India small given the resources devoted to this cause over 150 years. Arguably missionaries exerted far more influence in setting up schools and hospitals than they did in direct proselytising. Schools gave access to new cultural capitals of language and knowledge useful in the developing colonial capitalist political economy. Western medicine, often only accessible through medical missions given the paucity of investment by the colonial state in such matters of well-being, were valued by Indians of all religious and political persuasions.

Indian resistance to the persuasions of evangelical Christianity was rooted in the complex social formations of religion, politics and economy that shaped Indian society, through caste and other mechanisms of social differentiation and governmentality. However, the vocal castigation of Indian belief systems as heathen and practices of caste, child marriage and suttee (widow burning) as barbaric, at the same time as British colonial administrators entrenched a Brahminised version of Hinduism in juridical and legislative systems, invited a complex response from Indians of all faiths. As Chapter 2 discusses, one such reaction within Hinduism was the Brahmo Samaj (1865-) and the Arya Samaj (1875-). These reformers were able to relate to those fringe elements of European religious thought such as the Unitarians and Theosophists, who exhibited more open and egalitarian behaviours than mainstream imperial Christianity.

By the early twentieth century, Indian Christians themselves were becoming highly critical of the racialised arrogance of missionaries, pointing out the marked contradictions between Christian teachings and such behaviour. More progressive missionaries were themselves questioning old ways. In the following decades, progressive missions fostered indigenous leadership, and greater respect for religions such as Hinduism, Islam and Buddhism.[26] Some came to see the call for home rule, even full independence, as an eventual and desirable destiny for this greatest of British colonies.

A Post-colonial History of Colonialism

This book contributes to the post-colonial endeavour to make parochial a Eurocentric understanding of colonial history and its legacies.[27] We do so, however, not from the stance of post-colonial subjects. As scholars we are each positioned within post-empire constructions of whiteness and Western identity, albeit complicated through those very mobilities of empire that shape many of our historical subjects lives.[28] However, we each bring to this volume a deep engagement with colonial pasts as historians of gender, race and colonialism. This pre-figured our growing awareness that in the cracks and crevices of the colonial contact zone bordered by imperial Christianity, faith-based cross-cultural networks of affect and agency were shaping new patterns of civility and co-existence. These networks, as the case studies considered here reveal, not only straddle the colonial divides of race and creed, but also challenge some of the assumptions built into our own historical understanding of what it meant to be 'anti-colonial' or 'cosmopolitan' during this period. Such understandings are often derived either from the records and activities of states, great leaders and large international organisations or from evidence of subaltern mobilities and engagements. Here, we trace the lives of people neither plebeian nor famous; conservative or radical. Some fit the 'colonised subject' tag, and others, the 'coloniser'. But all were active in webs of connection, voluntary associations and activism that helped open up new ways of talking and thinking about cosmopolitan co-existence and showed these dual categories to be not only interrelated but interpersonally experienced as well.[29]

As we show in this book, race assumes myriad forms in interpersonal dialogues and exchanges across racial divides. Our focus on the diverse cosmopolitanisms articulated within liberal transnational networks of faith is not intended to reduce or ignore the centrality of race and especially hegemonic whiteness, underpinning the spaces and subjectivities these networks formed within and through. Rather, we seek to explore how new forms of cosmopolitanism could be articulated despite the awkward complicities and liminalities individuals and cosmopolitan thought zones inhabited. It is exactly this complexity between authentic otherness and universal sameness that energises the individuals and networks described in the following pages, and, we hope, our writing of them.

Notes

1. William E. B. Du Bois and Brent H. Edwards, *The Souls of Black Folk Oxford World's Classics* (Oxford: Oxford University Press, 2007), 3.
2. Vedanayakam Samuel Azariah, 'The Problem of Co-operation between Foreign and Native Workers,' in *World Missionary Conference, 1910: The History and Records of the Conference: Together with Addresses Delivered in the Evening Meetings* (Edinburgh, 1910), 315.
3. Stuart Hall, 'Culture, community, nation,' *Cultural Studies* 7, 3 (1993): 361.
4. See for example: John Maynard, 'Marching to a Different Beat: The Influence of the International Black Diaspora on Aboriginal Australia,' in *Indigenous Networks: Mobility, Connections and Exchange*, eds. Jane Carey and Jane Lydon. Routledge Studies in Cultural History 29 (New York: Routledge, 2014), 262–272. Margaret Allen, 'Friends alongside": Feminist Inter-cultural Co-operation in Kolkata in Early Twentieth Century', *Australian Feminist Studies,* 25, 66 (2010): 463–473. David Lambert and Alan Lester, eds. *Colonial Lives Across the British Empire: Imperial Careering in the Long Nineteenth Century* (Cambridge & New York: Cambridge University Press, 2006); Zoë Laidlaw, 'Breaking Britannia's Bounds? Law, Settlers, and Space In Britain's Imperial Historiography,' *The Historical Journal*, 55, 3 (2012): 807–30. Zoë Laidlaw, 'Indigenous Interlocutors: Networks of Imperial

Protest and Humanitarianism in the Mid-Nineteenth Century,' in *Indigenous Networks. Mobility, Connections and Exchange*, eds. Jane Carey and Jane Lydon. Routledge Studies in Cultural History 29 (New York: Routledge, 2014), 114–139.

5. Sugata Bose *A Hundred Horizons. The Indian Ocean in the Age of Global Imperialism* (Cambridge, MA: Harvard University Press, 2005). *Green, N.* 'Saints, Rebels and Booksellers: Sufis in the Cosmopolitan Western Indian Ocean, ca.1780–1920,' In *Struggling with History. Islam and Cosmopolitanism in the Western Indian* Ocean, eds E Simpson and K. Kresse (New York: Columbia University Press and Hurst: 2008): 125–66.
6. Sugata Bose and Kris Manjapra (eds), *Cosmopolitan Thought Zones. South Asia and the Global Circulation of Ideas* (Basingstoke: Palgrave Macmillan, 2010).
7. Kris Manjapra, 'Introduction'in *Cosmopolitan Thought Zones:2.*
8. Mrinalini Sinha, *Specters of Mother India: The Global Restructuring of an Empire* (Durham: Duke University Press, 2006).
9. Jonathan Schneer, *London 1900 The Imperial Metropolis* (New Haven: Yale University Press, 1999).
10. Satadru Sen, 'The Migrant's Empire: Loyalty and Imperial Citizenship at the League of Nations,' in *Rediscovering the British World*, eds. Phillip Buckner, R. Douglas Francis (Calgary: Calgary University Press, 2005), 305–319.
11. Nico Slate, *Colored Cosmopolitanism The Shared Struggle for Freedom in the United States and India* (Cambridge: Harvard University Press, 2011).
12. Tracey Banivanua Mar, *Decolonisation and the Pacific. Indigenous Globalisation and the Ends of Empire* (Cambridge: Cambridge University Press, 2016).
13. Ibid: 232.
14. Dipesh Chakrabarty, *Provincializing Europe Postcolonial Thought and Historical Difference.* Princeton Studies in Culture/Power/History (Princeton, NJ: Princeton University Press, 2000). Marilyn Lake, 'Chinese Colonists Assert Their 'Common Human Rights': Cosmopolitan as Subject and Method of History,' *Journal of World History* 21, 3 (2010): 375–92. Marilyn Lake, 'Chinese Warnings and White Men's Prophesies', in *Critical Perspectives on Colonialism: Writing the Empire from Below*, eds. Fiona Paisley and Kirsty Reid(New York: Routledge, 2014).
15. Melissa Gregg and Gregory J. Seigworth (eds),*The Affect Theory Reader* (Durham: Duke University Press, 2010).
16. Leela Gandhi, *Affective Communities: Anticolonial Thought, Fin-de-Siècle Radicalism, and the politics of friendship* (Durham and London: Duke University Press, 2006), 14.
17. Jane Haggis and Margaret Allen, 'Imperial Emotions: Affective communities of Mission in British Protestant Women's Missionary Publications

c1880–1920', *Journal of Social History* (Spring 2008) 41, 3: 691–716; Margaret Allen and Jane Haggis. 'True Friends or False? The Changing Nature of Relationships Between Indian and British Missionary Women in the Imperial Contact Zone of India, c1880–1940', *Outskirts*, 28 (May 2013) at http://www.outskirts.arts.uwa.edu.au/volumes/volume-28/margaret-allen-and-jane-haggis.

18. Clare Midgley, 'Transoceanic Commemoration and Connections Between Bengali Brahmos and British and American Unitarians,' *Historical Journal*, 54, 3 (2011): 801–824. Clare Midgley, 'Liberal Religion and the "woman question" Between East and West: Perspectives from a Bengali Women's Journal,' *Gender & History*, 25, 3 (2013):445–460; Clare Midgley, 'Mary Carpenter and the Brahmo Samaj of India: A Transnational Perspective on Social Reform in the Age of Empire', *Women's History Review*, 22, 2 (2013) 363–386.
19. Fiona Paisley. 'Glamour in the Pacific: Cultural Internationalism and Maori Politics at Pan-Pacific Women's Conferences in the 1950s', *Pacific Studies*, 29, 1/2 (December 2006): 54–81; Fiona Paisley, *Glamour in the Pacific: Cultural Internationalism and Race Politics in the Women's Pan-Pacific* (Honolulu: University of Hawaii Press, 2009).
20. Manjapra, 'Introduction,' 5.
21. Hugh Tinker, *A New System of Slavery: The Export of Indian Labour Overseas 1820–1920* (London: Oxford University Press, 1974).
22. Lata Mani, *Contentious Traditions: The Debate on Sati in Colonial India* (Berkeley: University of California Press, 1998); Partha Chatterjee, *Nationalist Thought and the Colonial World: A Derivative Discourse* (Minneapolis: University of Minnesota Press, 1993).
23. Gandhi, *Affective Communities.*
24. Ibid; Robert J. Holton, 'Cosmopolitanism or Cosmopolitanisms: The Universal Races Congress of 1911', *Global Networks,* 2, 2 (2002), 153–170; Slate, *Colored Cosmopolitanism*; Bose and Manjapra, *Cosmopolitan Thought Zones.*
25. Andrew May, *Welsh Missionaries and British Imperialism. The Empire of Clouds in North-East India* (Manchester: Manchester University Press, 2012).Andrew Porter, 'Religion, Missionary Enthusiasm, and Empire,' in *The Oxford History of the British Empire, Vol. III The Nineteenth Century,* ed. Andrew Porter, ed. in Chief: Wm Roger Louis. (Oxford: Oxford University Press, 2001), 222–246; Andrew Porter, 'Cultural Imperialism' and Protestant Missionary Enterprise, 1780–1914,' *Journal of Imperial and Commonwealth History*, XXV, 3 (1997): 367–391. Brian Stanley, *The Bible and the Flag: Protestant Missions and British Imperialism in Nineteenth and Twentieth Centuries* (Apollos: Leicester, UK, 1990).
26. Margaret Sinclair, *William Paton* (London: SCM Press, 1949), 28.

27. Chakrabarty, *Provincializing Europe.*
28. Jane Haggis, 'Situated Knowledge or Ego (His)toire?: Memory, History and the She-Migrant in an Imaginary of "Terra Nullius"', in *Ngapartji Ngapartji In Turn, In Turn: Ego-Histoire, Europe and Indigenous Australia,* eds. Vanessa Castejon, Anna Cole, Oliver Haag and Karen Hughes (Canberra: ANU Press,2014), 159–172. Jane Haggis and Susanne Schech, 'Meaning Well and Global Good Manners: Reflections on White Western Feminist Cross-cultural Praxis,' *Australian Feminist Studies,* 15, 33 (2000): 387–399; Jane Haggis, 'White Australia and Otherness: The Limits to Hospitality,' in *Cultures in Refuge. Seeking Sanctuary in Modern Australia*, eds. Anna Hayes and Robert Mason (1st ed. Ashgate Publishing, 2012; 2nd ed. Abingdon and New York: Routledge, 2016), 15–30.
29. Lisa Lowe, *The Intimacies of Four Continents* (Durham: Duke University Press, 2015), Gopalan Balachandran, 'Circulation Through Seafaring: Indian Seamen, 1890–1945', in *Society and Circulation: Mobile People and Itinerant Cultures in South Asia 1750–1950*, eds. Claude Markovits, Jacques Pouchepadass and Sanjay Subrahmanyam (Delhi: Permanent Black, 2003), 88–130.

CHAPTER 2

The Cosmopolitan Biography of the English Religious Liberal, Feminist and Writer, Sophia Dobson Collet

Introduction: Representing Cosmopolitan Lives

Abstract This chapter explores the cosmopolitan life of the little-known English religious liberal, feminist and writer, Sophia Dobson Collet (1822–1894). It examines Collet's close connection with members of the Brahmo Samaj, a movement founded in 1820s Calcutta by Ram Mohan Roy to promote religious and social reform among Hindus. It shows her pivotal role in shaping a 'cosmopolitan thought zone' connecting Brahmos with British and American Unitarians, Transcendentalists, Theists and liberal Christians. Collet, it argues, enacted spiritual fellowship and a shared commitment to social reform within a respectful trans-racial and trans-faith affective community. Although she did not articulate an anti-imperial politics, she was committed to bridging the racialised divisions and hierarchies that characterised the 'imperial social formation' between Britain and India.

Keywords Sophia Dobson Collet · Brahmo Samaj · Spiritual cosmopolitanism · Cosmopolitan feminism · Affective community · Unitarianism

In June 1894 a seven-page obituary of the English religious liberal, feminist and writer Sophia Dobson Collet (1822–1894) appeared in the Bengali-language publication *Bamabodhini Patrika* [*Journal for the Enlightenment of Women*]. Describing Collet as 'India's dearest friend and well-wisher', it was noted that she 'kept on mentioning how much

J. Haggis et al., *Cosmopolitan Lives on the Cusp of Empire*,
DOI 10.1007/978-3-319-52748-2_2

she wanted to finish writing the biography of Rajah Rammohan Roy before she died'.[1] The article went on to describe Collet as 'one of the noted scholars and learned women of her time' and to emphasise her important role in promoting the Brahmo Samaj. This was an influential Indian movement for religious and social reform which Ram Mohan Roy had founded in the 1820s in Calcutta, and of which the male editors of the journal were currently the leading members.[2]

Collet's *The Life and Letters of Raja Rammohun Roy* was finally published in 1900 after its completion by her friend. It became the standard English-language biography of this 'father of modern India', who had already become an international celebrity during his lifetime.[3] Collet herself has, in contrast, remained an obscure figure, and is now unknown beyond a small circle of scholars interested in the role of religious radicals in the emergence of feminism in Britain.[4] The significance of her close involvement with Indian reformers over a 30-year period awaits detailed study, while the most extensive biographical account of her life to date is in the form of a prefix inserted into the 1913 Calcutta edition of her *Life and Letters of Raja Rammohun Roy*.[5] The difference in the public status of the two figures whose lives appear in the 1913 book is poignantly brought home by the contrast between the two images accompanying the two biographies: reproductions of a tiny sketch portrait bust of Collet (see Fig. 2.1), and a grand full-length oil portrait of Roy commissioned by one of his English women admirers.

This chapter focusses on the 'life and letters' of this English woman who devoted so many years of her life to researching Roy's life. It presents her as a woman with a cosmopolitan outlook who sought to bridge the gendered and racialised divisions and hierarchies that characterised the 'imperial social formation' between Britain and India.[6]

In interpreting Collet's close relationships with the Indian religious and social reformers of the Brahmo Samaj, I have found helpful Bose and Manjapra's concept of 'aspirational cosmopolitanism', which they define as 'the pursuit of conversations across lines of difference, between disparate socio-cultural, political and linguistic groups, that provisionally created shared public worlds'. They define such 'shared transnational public spaces' as 'cosmopolitan thought zones' which were 'marked by irreducible incongruities of power and cultural values, yet also by a degree of shared dwelling' based on a search to 'solve problems together'.[7] Collet's close connection with the Brahmo Samaj, and the wider history of transnational connection, interchange, friendship and practical collaboration

Fig. 2.1 Portrait Drawing of Sophie Dobson Collet

Source: H.C. Sarkar, ed., *Life and Letters of Raja Rammohun Roy by Sophia Dobson Collet* (Calcutta: A.C. Sarkar at the B.M. Press, 1913).

on matters of religion and social reform between Indian members of the various branches of the Brahmo Samaj on the one hand, and a loosely knit community of British and American Unitarians, Transcendentalists, Theists and liberal Christians on the other, provides a sustained example of this phenomenon.[8] While Brahmoism began as a movement to reform Hinduism from within, and Unitarianism and Transcendentalism were rooted in Protestant Christianity, connection across faith boundaries was articulated as a sense of 'spiritual fellowship' transcending cultural differences, and a feeling of being 'kindred spirits' – what we might usefully label spiritual cosmopolitanism. It also involved a sense of mutual inspiration in matters of social reform, including a shared commitment to improve the position of women. As English Unitarian poet and feminist Lucy Aikin wrote to leading American Unitarian minister William Ellery Channing in 1831 after meeting with Ram Mohan Roy: 'Just now my feelings are more cosmopolite than usual; I take a personal concern in a *third* quarter of the globe, since I have seen the excellent Ram-Mohun-Roy'.[9]

Bose and Manjapra open up a useful analytical space for considering the web of connection which Collet helped to weave between the Unitarians and Brahmo Samaj. They emphasise how cosmopolitanism in the context of South Asia in the colonial period was an ethical project complementing the political project of nationalist resistance. While the Brahmo-Unitarian network did not directly challenge imperial power relations at the level of governance, it operated as a voluntary web of association outside official colonial networks. The network promoted forms of respectful cross-cultural and inter-faith exchange that undermined racist cultural attitudes and social structures; it also explicitly challenged missionary imperialism and offered a model of inter-faith cooperation as an alternative to the polarisation between orthodox Hindus and evangelical Christians.[10]

There are, however, limits to the applicability of Bose and Manjapra's existing model of aspirational cosmopolitanism to understand Collet's life and the broader history of Brahmo-Unitarian connections. This chapter argues for the value of a more capacious definition of cosmopolitanism. In particular, it calls into question the primacy accorded to shared *public* space and *public* worlds in Bose and Manjapra's definition. Such a primacy ignores the gendered nature of public spheres in the nineteenth century and results in an unproblematised focus on male actors. Leela Gandhi's concept of 'affective communities' offers a useful antidote to this, bringing to the fore the more intimate dimensions of cosmopolitanism as a 'politics of friendship' characterised by 'affective gestures that refuse alignment along the secure axes of filiation to seek expression outside, if not against, possessive communities of belonging'.[11] As this chapter will show, Collet's life vividly demonstrates that it was the interplay between the intimate, domestic and affective world of friendship, hospitality and personal support and the global circulation of ideas in the public world of religious and social reform that was crucial to 'spiritual cosmopolitanism'. As such, it fits well with an influential recent definition of cosmopolitanism as 'thinking and feeling beyond the nation'.[12]

Another aspect of aspirational cosmopolitanism that is ignored by Bose and Manjapra is the differences in the ways in which members of a transnational network might position themselves, and be positioned by others, as cosmopolitan in the context of their gendered and racialised positioning. Insight into this complexity is gained if we compare representations of the cosmopolitan identity of Collet with that of her close friend, the charismatic leader of the Brahmo Samaj, Keshub Chunder Sen. On his visit to England in 1870, Sen asserted a masculine cosmopolitan identity, implicitly challenging the colonial denigration of the 'effeminate Bengali' by describing himself as 'a man of the world' in his farewell address to the British and Foreign Unitarian Association.[13] In a fascinating mirroring of the universalising language of Victorian Protestant missionaries, this identification was made on the basis of a new understanding of the place of his theist spiritual beliefs in the world:

> On the banks of the Thames, as on the banks of the Ganges, I have opened the secrets of my aspiration and prayers to the one loving and holy God, and He has heard me here as He did there . . . I am now, thank God, a man of the world, and can say that England is as much my Father's house as India.[14]

In this statement, Sen publicly presented a masculine cosmopolitan identity as developed through overseas travel, public prayer and recognition of religious universalism. In contrast, Collet's cosmopolitanism is represented in her obituary in the Brahmo *Journal for the Enlightenment of Women* thus:

> [H]er love and affection for India shaped up in a way that she soon started feeling one with the millions of Indians – she suffered at their pain, smiled at their happiness. Just as the British living in India waited for that one letter from Britain, she waited for her Indian friends to write to her. Often those

> close to her would ask whether she had an update from her home, i.e. India. In spite of being a Christian herself, she took up the cause and the movement of the Brahma-Samaj as her own, and helped spread its ideas through her work.[15]

Here, Collet's cosmopolitanism is presented as an internal process of self-identification with India and Indians, which was rooted not in physical travel overseas but rather in the cultivation of friendships and exchange of private correspondence. Her promotion of the Brahmo Samaj is presented as being based on her respect for a different faith rather than a religious universalism. The challenge to colonial discourse also comes from a different direction. While Sen states that he has come to realise through travel that his theism means he can be at home in the imperial metropole, Collet is described as identifying India as her home despite never having travelled there from her London home. Any necessary correlation between overseas travel and the development of a cosmopolitan outlook is challenged by contrasting her to English colonial 'ex-pats' living in India, who continue to see England as their home. The contrast between the cosmopolitan positioning of these leading members of a transnational network of religious liberals and social reformers alerts us to the varied ways in which cosmopolitanism could be articulated. This is a useful starting point for the fuller exploration of the nature of Collet's cosmopolitanism which forms the focus of this chapter.

In analysing Collet's cosmopolitanism, this chapter adopts a transnational perspective that seeks to bridge the gap between the two existing biographical sketches of her life: Brahmo activist Hem Chandra Sarkar's prefix to the 1913 edition of her *Life and Letters of Raja Rammohun Roy*, and English feminist historian Kathryn Gleadle's entry on Collet for the 2004 *Oxford Dictionary of National Biography*. Sarkar presents India as the focus of Collet's life work and emotional energies and asserts that 'The Brahmo Samaj was uppermost in her heart and mind'.[16] In contrast, Gleadle, though she includes a paragraph on her support for the Brahmo Samaj, concentrates on Collet's life as a journalist, a feminist, a supporter of Chartism, a promoter of peace and anti-vivisection, and a religious liberal within a British context.[17] Bringing together Collet's Indian, British and broader transnational engagements, the chapter discusses her religious cosmopolitanism as a search for affective religious community, draws out her significance as a cosmopolitan writer on religion, and shows how her religious cosmopolitanism influenced her feminism.

In conclusion, it addresses the implications of this case study for our broader understanding of the nature of cosmopolitanisms emerging out of imperial contact zones.

Collet's Religious Cosmopolitanism as a Search for Affective Religious Community

As Sarkar notes in his biographical sketch, Collet 'passed through many and interesting phases of religious experience', though remaining 'always very broad and liberal'.[18] As a child, her involvement with the radical Unitarian congregation at South Place Chapel in London in the 1830s brought her into contact with Ram Mohan Roy, who came to speak at the chapel, making her aware of a liberal religious movement which was developing from Hindu rather than from Christian roots. On Roy's death in Bristol in 1833, the minister of South Place, W.J. Fox, delivered a sermon in Roy's honour. Collet later listed the published version of this as one of her sources for her *Life and Letters of Raja Rammohun Roy*.[19] Sarkar describes Collet's devotion to the Brahmo Samaj as 'almost of the nature of a romance' and roots it in this childhood encounter: 'Impressed by the magnetic personality of the founder of the Brahmo Samaj . . . she remained a most loyal and devoted supporter of the church throughout its life'.[20]

Collet remained an active member of South Place Chapel into the 1840s.[21] This also drew her into transatlantic Unitarian religious and reform networks: She became part of circles influenced by Ralph Waldo Emerson, a leading American Transcendentalist. As a result, she started to move beyond Christianity, with its stress on the authority of the Bible, to a more intuitive form of theism.[22] Transcendentalist beliefs were influenced by Eastern spiritual traditions. Emerson, whose series of London lectures Collet enthusiastically attended in 1848, was a leading promoter of cosmopolitanism. Indeed, on attending his lectures, Collet was getting a flavour of the antebellum New England lyceum lecture circuit. This was an important arena within which women, denied full national citizenship rights, were encouraged to imagine themselves as 'citizens of the world' through developing a relativist outlook towards other cultures and an ethical sense of obligation to strangers.[23]

Collet was also influenced by the more extreme Freethinking and Secularist speakers to whom South Place offered a platform. She wrote articles for the atheist and socialist George Jacob Holyoake's periodicals in the 1840 and 1850s under the pseudonym 'Panthea'.[24] Further suggesting her developing cosmopolitan outlook at this time, in a letter to her aunt Mary, an orthodox Christian who was horrified by her religious heterodoxy, Collet linked her pantheistic belief that God was 'immanent in all spirit and all space' to a globalised, non-Eurocentric geographical vision. She stated that she would protest against 'equating religion and morality with Christianity' just as she would 'protest against calling the wide ocean by the name of the British Channel just because that is the part of it best known and appreciated by us'.[25]

By 1857, however, Collet, as her surviving manuscript 'Intellectual Diary' for that year reveals, was considering a return to the Unitarian Christian beliefs of her childhood. This was partly the result of her enthusiasm for the heartfelt form of Unitarianism espoused by the leading British minister James Martineau. It was also partly because of her discontent with the religious writings of leading Transcendentalists, which she felt were too abstract and 'wholly unable to realise the special truths incarnated in any other doctrine, or be conscious of the spirit needs which gave to many mediate forms of truth their hold on the human heart'. Collet's valuing of different spiritual traditions developed in diverse cultural contexts anticipates the grounds of her later engagement with the Brahmo Samaj.[26] We might describe her distinctive stance as one of spiritual cosmopolitanism rather than religious universalism.[27]

By 1861, Collet had definitively moved away from 'pure' theism: She later described her 'conversion to Christianity' as having taken place in that year.[28] Initially returning to Unitarianism, she was then attracted to Christian Socialism; finally, in 1870, she was baptised at an Anglican church and became a Trinitarian Christian.[29] This move did not, however, represent a retreat into narrow religious orthodoxy.[30] For, at the same time as her personal beliefs were moving away from Transcendentalist theism towards mainstream Protestantism, she was becoming intensely interested in news of the development of a new theist movement in India. She learned of this through the medium of her theist friends Frances Power Cobbe and Francis W. Newman, who wrote informing her about the revival of the Brahmo Samaj under Keshub Chunder Sen.[31]

Cobbe, as a theist, aligned her religious position to the Brahmos to the extent of describing herself as a 'Brahmika' (female member of the Brahmo Samaj).[32] In contrast, Collet forged her own connection with Brahmos as a Christian who belonged to a *different* religion but who felt a sense of close spiritual *affinity*. As she stated in a letter published in 1870 in the Brahmo *Journal for the Enlightenment of Women*:

> Even if I am a Christian, I feel immense love and respect for the *Brahmos*. The prayers that I heard here of your religion, I look forward to do the same in Calcutta at the temple of your religion. If that does not happen, I hope to meet you in God's lovely garden one day and live there as a family.[33]

Her use of familial imagery paints a domestic-based and heart-felt cosmopolitan vision of heaven as a site of cross-cultural and inter-faith unity, a vision which stood in sharp contrast to the standard Christian belief that only Christian converts would go to heaven and broke sharply with evangelical Protestant missionary discourse which linked the heavenly family to the patriarchal English missionary family, whose role it was to parent racialised others and lead them to God.[34]

Collet's language suggests her deep longing for spiritual community at this time. It is clear that, in her life-long determination to chart her own faith path, she struggled to find a religious community in England to which she felt she truly belonged. In a heartfelt passage to an English friend, she later recalled:

> [M]y mother and aunt, and all my brothers and sisters (or belles-soeurs) except Collet, held aloof when there was anything seriously unpopular about my heroes or favourites – Still I pulled on, somehow – at last I became a Christian, to the amazement of all my friends. Then a new bond arose, and a new enthusiasm, and the tables were turned to some slight extent. Next came India and the B. Samaj, bringing a fresh recast of mental relationships.[35]

Collet continued: 'All these developments had resulted in a curiously heterogeneous field of friendships and associations, wh. had, however, no antagonistic elements. . . .'[36] Her cosmopolitanism was characterised by this valuing of harmonious heterogeneity within her affective community.

Collet's discovery of the revived Brahmo Samaj was life-changing: it provided her with a focus for her future life and work as she took on the role of promoting the movement to the British public. As a single middle-class woman in her 30s, Collet had longed for a purpose beyond a traditional focus on marriage and motherhood, as she had recorded in her Intellectual Diary of 5 March 1857:

> [T]hose graceful woman-novels, 'Florence Templar, 'Thorney Hall', etc. they are merely autobiographies of the affections *purs et simples*. The heroines love . . . but . . . they have no life of their own – no purpose beyond the affections, no aspirations except a vague desire to be good. How can women be so easily contented – so torpid? Oh! For strength to live out something fuller and nobler without forgetting the restraining grace of womanhood.[37]

In this context, her intellectual, spiritual and emotional engagement over a period of 30 years with the Brahmo Samaj can be seen as a cosmopolitan-oriented resolution of what she described elsewhere in her Intellectual Diary as 'the full problem of women's deep nature . . . – the problem namely, of fusing intellect, passion, and action, in the purest flow of the religious and human affections'.[38]

While Collet never fulfilled her dream of travelling to Calcutta, she began to correspond with Sen after being put in in touch with him by Cobbe and Newman in 1869. She subsequently was crucial in insuring the success of Sen's visit to Britain in 1870. Indeed, her Bengali biographer Sarkar claimed that 'much of the success of Mr Sen's English visit and the warm reception accorded to him was due to the efforts of Miss Collet'.[39] A private letter that Sen wrote to Collet in 1874 gives a sense of the intimacy that developed between them during and following his visit, and suggests how highly Sen valued Collet's moral support. Addressed to 'My dear friend' and signed 'With love ever yours affectionately Keshub Chunder Sen', it told her that his children 'eagerly await' the presents she is sending to them through his close Brahmo colleague Protap Mozomdar, who was returning to Bengal following a visit to Britain, and expressed thanks for her 'words of sympathy and support' in an internal controversy within the Brahmo Samaj, and for sending him a 'beautiful picture' of 'Consolation'.[40]

Following Sen's visit, Collet also entered into correspondence with other leading male and female members of the Brahmo Samaj, fostering a broader 'affective community' rooted in a sense of spiritual fellowship. Her first letter to a Brahmo woman, published in translation in *Bamabodhini Patrika* in 1870, gives a vivid sense of how she saw friendship as the basis for cross-cultural community and helps us better understand the reference to Collet's 'Indian home' in her obituary. Her letter began by expressing the wish that her (unnamed) correspondent could be a neighbour, rather than living so far away, as she would have loved to have visited her home and find out about her domestic life: 'If you were not living so far away from me I would have been very pleased. We could have had pleasant conversations and would have come to know about your life in the *antahpur* [women's quarters]and your children'.[41] This genuine interest in a Bengali woman's domestic life contrasts with the constant repetition in Christian missionary writings of the horrors of the dark, dirty and confining space of the women's quarters of the Bengali home. To foster her correspondence with Brahmo women, she learned Bengali. As Sarkar notes: 'She used to write in Bengali very affectionately to many Brahmo ladies whom she had never seen'.[42]

Sarkar also draws attention to Collet's 'warm reception of, and valuable help to' Indians who visited England from the time of the visit of Keshub Chunder Sen right down to the date of her death. Brahmo gentlemen in London, he states, 'found in her a most kind friend and well-wisher, ever ready to assist them with sound advice and guidance'. He quotes from a letter written to Collet by Ananda Mohan Bose when leaving England in 1874 at the end of a four-year stay to train at Cambridge as a barrister, which emphasised 'the happiness and pleasure I have derived from your acquaintance and friendship' and noted that, in the days he spent with her, he 'derived a strengthening and cheering influence from your example and words'.[43] Collet also lent her support to Indian feminist Pandita Ramabai, a convert from Brahmoism to Unitarian Christianity, during her stay in Britain in the 1880s, sending her publications by the Brahmo Samaj.[44]

Collet as a Cosmopolitan Writer on Religion

In the decade prior to the beginnings of her engagement with the Brahmo Samaj, Collet had already gained a considerable public profile in Britain and the USA as a writer on religious matters from a theist perspective, and the study of these earlier writings gives insights into the roots of her cosmopolitan approach to religion. In particular, her writings in the 1850s on the life and ideas of the leading British secularist George Jacob Holyoake were marked by a sympathetic engagement across the theist-atheist divide which demonstrated an open-minded engagement with difference. Her assertion that 'rival systems do not stand to each other in the relation of absolute truth and absolute falsehood, but as different conceptions of truth'[45] fore-shadowed her later approach to engaging as a liberal Christian with the Brahmo Samaj.

This public engagement began with an article in the *Contemporary Review* of February 1870 on 'Indian Theism and its Relation to Christianity', which she then revised and published in pamphlet form.[46] The pamphlet sought to explain the religious position of Sen to the British public. Urging them to welcome him on his visit to England, Collet argued that it was perfectly consistent for him to hold up Jesus as a bond of connection between East and West and the greatest benefactor of mankind without pledging himself to Trinitarian theology or forgetting his own Theist doctrine. Brahmos, she explained, were thirsting for God who was 'God without a second', and this was the 'indispensable foundation of all religion'.[47] While acknowledging that Brahmoism might perhaps in the future provide a bridge between Hinduism and Christianity, she warned that attempting to convert Brahmos to Christianity was inappropriate: they were already doing essential work for God and rescuing hundreds of souls from heathen bondage. She concluded: 'Let us not, then refuse our Christian sympathies to these Hindoo Unitarians, as fellow-worshippers of our common Father, fellow-learners of the teaching of His Son, fellow-seekers of the Kingdom of Heaven.'[48]

Collet was also keen to spread knowledge of the Brahmo Samaj beyond Britain, and she made connections with continental European liberal Christian theologists who were interested in Sen's work. She wrote a *Historical Sketch of the Brahmo Samaj* at the request of Dr Max Krenkel of Dresden, as an introduction to a German translation he was publishing of Sen's lectures and tracts. At the request of her Brahmo friends, she then arranged to publish it in Calcutta in its original English form in 1873, in an interesting instance of the transnational and trans-lingual circulation of texts that was a feature of aspirational cosmopolitanism. In her preface to this version, she emphasised that common ground with Indian Theists was not confined to heterodox Unitarian Christians:

> I am a Trinitarian Christian, and not a member of the Brahmo Samaj. But I feel strongly that all earnest believers in a Personal and Perfect God hold so much vital truth in common, that Christians and Theists, without the slightest unfaithfulness to their separate differences of conviction, may and should cooperate largely for the promotion of truth and righteousness, and the abatement of heathenism and unbelief.[49]

The Brahmo Samaj was deserving of Western support, she argued, as 'a true Church of God' which was 'doing a real and most sacred work for Him in a country which the West has, as yet, failed to Christianize'.[50]

Collet took on the key role of record keeper for the contemporary movement of Brahmo Samaj. She recorded and circulated information on its activities and published a detailed record of Sen's time in England, *Keshub Chunder Sen's English Visit*.[51] Between 1876 and 1882, she compiled a set of *Brahmo Year Books* recording the activities of the various branches of the movement all over India. Her introductory description of the purpose of these yearbooks clearly articulated the perspective of aspirational spiritual cosmopolitanism that she brought to the project. Her aim, she stated, was to foster 'the mutual interchange of spiritual experience' across religious and ethnic boundaries. This she rooted in her belief that: 'the practical Christian and the devout Theist (whether Jew or Brahmo, Asiatic or Saxon) have each lessons to learn from the other; they already hold far more in common than either is wont to suspect'.[52] Echoing earlier Unitarian writings, and in direct opposition to evangelical missionaries, Collet made it clear that she was convinced that only indigenous movements such as the Brahmo Samaj could bring about a religious reformation in India. But she went further than this: She also challenged the belief that all progressive movements originated in the West by expressing the hope that the movement's 'fervour of devotion joined to the simplicity of creed' could be a 'means of grace' to all those in the West 'who find established forms uncongenial, and the popular theologies incredible'.[53] She clearly had in mind her friends who were Transcendentalists and theists, and she sent the yearbook to leading Unitarians in the USA.[54]

Having been a prominent supporter of Sen's Indian theism, Collet became disillusioned with the new direction in which Sen sought to lead the Brahmo Samaj in the late 1870s. She was convinced that he was moving away from the founding principles of Brahmoism, with its commitment to the radical religious and social reform of Hindu culture. Her aspirational spiritual cosmopolitanism was never based on uncritical cultural relativism, and she publicly attacked Sen's new religious vision of a universal and purified faith, arguing that it was based on the false premise that all established and orthodox religions were equally true and involved the reintroduction of unreformed Hindu religious practices, which had previously been rejected by Brahmo reformers.[55] This, she argued, was a backwards step to 'mental slavery, superstition, and idolatry' rather than a forward-looking move towards a 'pure, spiritual, enlightened' religious life in India.[56] She also sought to combat the influence of Sen's new religious ideas beyond India, encouraging Westerners to instead throw their support behind his opponents in the Sadharan Brahmo Samaj, stating that her own religious position as a Christian was based on the same foundations as their 'pure theism'.[57]

Collet formed a close connection with the leader of this new organisation, Sivanath Sastri. When Sastri visited her in England in 1888, she persuaded him to write a full history of Brahmoism.[58] Perhaps keen to record that the roots of Brahmoism lay in a radical critique of orthodox Hinduism which was at odds with Sen's new position, she also shifted her own focus from compiling the yearbooks to researching an English-language biography of the revered founder of the movement, Ram Mohan Roy. It was a work that complemented the newly published Bengali-language life of Roy by Nagendra Nath Chatterji.[59] She worked on this book right up until her death in 1894, scrupulously researching and fact-checking to create a work that her own biographer, Sarkar, described as 'an ideal of conscientious biography'.[60] She included multiple quotes from Roy's own writings, allowing him to speak for himself to the reader, as had been her approach in her earlier study of the life and work of English secularist George Holyoke.[61]

Collet's account of Roy's religious development presented him as a truly cosmopolitan intellectual rather than a man simply influenced by the influx of Western or Christian ideas into India following the imposition of British colonial rule. She explained that he had learned many languages in order to read diverse religious texts in their original and that his own beliefs drew on several religious traditions, including Hinduism, Buddhism and Islam as well as Christianity.[62] She presented Roy not as a convert to Unitarian Christianity, as some of his Western supporters had earlier tried to claim, but as a reformer of Hinduism who attempted to eradicate idolatrous practices and return to its earlier pure form.[63]

Collet's Cosmopolitan Feminism

Collet's deep attraction to Roy and to the Brahmo Samaj was not only based on a sense of spiritual affinity; it was also based on her approval as a feminist of the priority Roy and his movement gave to improving the position of Indian women. Her spiritual cosmopolitanism and her cosmopolitan feminism were inseparable, just as Roy's position as a religious and social reformer was inseparable. This is unsurprising, given her background. The radical Unitarian congregation in which she was involved in her youth was at the centre of the development of early feminist thought. In this milieu, commitment to improving the position of women was understood not simply as a Western or Christian prerogative. It could also involve reformist Indian men like Ram Mohan Roy, celebrated not only as a religious reformer but as the man responsible for the abolition of sati, the Hindu practice of burning alive widows on the funeral pyres of their husbands. Collet became one of a group of Freethinking feminists who challenged male religious authority and 'condemned the oppression of women in Scripture and the subordinate position assigned to them by Christianity'.[64] This was a stance which stood in sharp contrast to mainstream evangelical missionary and colonial discourse, which emphasised the privileges accorded to women in Christian nations and contrasted these with their oppression in 'heathen' lands. Collet's biography of Roy not only included a detailed discussion of his role in the abolition of sati but also emphasised the cosmopolitanism of his feminism, noting his 'thorough defence of women in general and Indian women in particular'.[65]

Collet's initial hero-worship of Sen in the 1870s was similarly based on her enthusiasm for his combination of religious reform with a commitment to social reform focussed on the position of women. She was also very excited to discover that Indian women were beginning to take initiatives of their own to improve the position of women, and she saw the 'pure faith' of Brahmoism as responsible for stimulating 'the female intelligence of India'.[66] She wrote in Bengali to Radharani Lahiri, secretary of Bama Hitohishini Shobha (the Women's Welfare Committee), to find out more about Brahmo women's own engagement with the 'woman question', stating that she was seeking the information in the spirit of 'appreciation and deep empathy for all of you who are devoting their time and energy for women's advancement in Bengal'.[67] As I have discussed elsewhere, Collet's engagement with Brahmo women activists shows a spirit of equal exchange on the 'woman question' rather than an imperial feminist assertion of her authority and power as a white woman to rescue victimised Indian women.[68]

Having actively supported Sen's controversial campaign against child marriage,[69] Collet was horrified when in 1878 he decided to marry his under-age daughter to the Maharajah of Cooch Behar. Her disillusion with Sen's new religious direction, discussed above, was intertwined with her anger at his betrayal of the Brahmo social reform agenda.[70] She then threw her support behind the Sadharan Brahmo Samaj both because she felt that it was adhering to true theism and because of its 'cordial recognition of the equal value of both sexes'[71] Her *Brahmo Year-Books* reported on its progressive initiatives in developing women's education, and detailed women's own organisational activities.[72]

In the mid-1880s, Collet found a way of directly linking her support for the British feminist movement with her support for Brahmo social reformers, to their mutual benefit. She was instrumental in connecting leaders of the Sadharan Brahmo Samaj to the journalist William Stead, who was the standing trial for his involvement in a controversial campaign against child prostitution in Britain, and to the outspoken feminist activist Josephine Butler. She helped persuade Butler to turn her attention to the abolition of the Contagious Diseases Act (C.D. Acts) in colonial India, following Butler's success in securing the repeal of the C.D. Acts as they applied to Britain.[73] As she explained in a letter to a friend, she was 'anxious to do all I can to bring Brahmo workers *en rapport* with English philanthropists and true Christians and no cause can be more vital than this'.[74]

Conclusion

What can this case study of the English religious liberal, feminist and writer Sophia Dobson Collet contribute to our broader understanding of the nature of cosmopolitanisms emerging out of imperial contact zones?

Collet's life throws new light on the informal transnational network comprising members of an influential Indian religious and social reform movement, the Brahmo Samaj, and British and American Unitarians and religious liberals. This network, initiated in the 1810s to 1830s, revived in the 1860s to 1880s, and persisting into the 1930s, comprised a triangular web of connection between British, American and Indian activists that intertwined imperial and transatlantic circuits of exchange. As this chapter has discussed, Collet's own religious liberalism and cosmopolitan outlook developed initially mainly within a transatlantic circuit of exchange among Unitarians and Transcendentalists, but already involved an awareness of religious and social reform in India through the figure of Ram Mohan Roy. Her cosmopolitanism was later enacted primarily within an imperial circuit involving links between members of the Brahmo Samaj and their

British supporters, but also encompassed the circulation of information on the Brahmo Samaj to Continental European and American religious liberals.

A cosmopolitan sensibility can take a variety of forms: it can involve fresh perspectives on the world gained through geographical travel or through an openness to new ideas; it can emphasise a stance of non-judgmental cultural relativism or be a quest for areas of common ground across lines of difference; it can involve the forging of cross-cultural friendships and exchanges across distance or involve an attempt to leave behind one's own original cultural identity though complete identification with another culture. Cosmopolitanism can operate at the level of intellectual engagement, spiritual connection, affective bonding or practical collaboration to bring about social or political change. Collet's own life is an example of sedentary cosmopolitanism, as she never visited India. It involved a quest for spiritual affinity across the lines of difference between liberal Christianity and Indian theism, which encompassed a shared critique of orthodox Hinduism rather than an espousal of cultural relativism. It was rooted in the cultivation of sustained and close friendships with Brahmo men and women, and this also involved her in some psychological repositioning, as reflected in the claim in her obituary that she referred to India, not Britain, as her home. Collet's cosmopolitanism combined intellectual, spiritual, affective and social activist dimensions. She saw promotion of the Brahmo Samaj as her life's work, and engaged over a period of over 20 years in the exchange of ideas with Brahmo friends on matters of religion, social reform and the position of women, diligently promoted the movement in the West through her writings, and put immense efforts into her role as record-keeper and historian and biographer of the movement and its leaders.

Collet's cosmopolitanism was certainly 'aspirational' in Bose and Manjapra's terms. She pursued conversations across lines of difference marked by race, ethnicity, religion, language, gender and nation, forging respectful egalitarian relationships across the coloniser/colonised divide. Her work with the Brahmo Samaj was a precursor to those ethical projects these scholars identify as complementing the political project of anti-colonialism at a slightly later date. However, Collet did not herself question Britain's right to exert its imperial rule over India. One explanation for this may be that some of Collet's own relatives had been employed by the East India Company. A second possibility is that her central preoccupation was with theology and that she was disinterested in imperial politics: it is noticeable that her 1857 intellectual diary makes no mention whatsoever of the Great Rebellion that shook Britain's imperial self-confidence, while devoting several pages to a detailed discussion of a book about India's ancient civilisations and religions. Third, Collet's long-distance relationship with Brahmos in India did not force her to directly confront the racism of colonial society; her hospitality to Indian men in the London metropole did not threaten colonial hierarchies in the way that attempts to cultivate cross-racial friendships within colonial India would have done. Finally, and perhaps crucially, Brahmos themselves were among the nineteenth-century Indian social reform groups who had no qualms about trying to use the legislative powers of the colonial government to advance their own agenda. Collet was clearly comfortable with this approach to bringing about social change in India: She urged the British government to support the Brahmo Marriage Act, and later sent copies of her Brahmo Year Books to the India Office. Keshub Chunder Sen himself stressed his loyalty to the British and his admiration for Queen Victoria. It is perhaps significant that Collet's attack on his decision to marry off his underage daughter to the Maharaja of Cooch Behar did not address the pressure that British colonial officials had put Sen under to agree to the marriage in order to advance their own strategic interests in the Princely State.[75]

Before the schism and decline in the movement caused by Sen's actions, the Brahmo-Unitarian connection, nurtured by Collet through the 1870s, provided an important alternative to the endemic conflict that characterised relationships between evangelical Christian missionaries and orthodox Hindu religious leaders. It was distinctive in being based on a sense of spiritual affinity among groups operating on the radical margins of Protestant Christian and Hindu religious traditions. Theosophy was a new form of spiritual cosmopolitan, which seems to have displaced and marginalised this Brahmo-Unitarian eastwest collaborative axis from the 1880s onwards. It gained an influential following among Indian nationalists and their Western supporters, as instanced by the two Theosophists who feature in the following chapters of this book. Such broadly anti-imperial Westerners who networked with anti-colonial nationalist elites were part of a later generation of 'freethinking intellectuals, social reformers and radicals'[76] than the one to which Collet belonged.

Notes

1. 'Sophia Dobson Collet', *Bamabodhini Patrika* [*Journal for the Enlightenment of Women*], 353 (June 1894), pp. 53–59. My thanks to Sahana Bajpaie for this and other translations from the journal used in this article.
2. D. Kopf, *The Brahmo Samaj and the Shaping of the Modern World* (New Delhi: Atlantic, 1996).
3. S. D. Collet, *The Life and Letters of Raja Rammohun Roy* (London: Harold Collet, 1900).
4. K. Gleadle, *The Early Feminists. Radical Unitarians and the Emergence of the Women's Rights Movement, 1831–51* (Basingstoke: Macmillan, 1995); L. Schwartz, *Infidel Feminism. Secularism, Religion and Women's Emancipation, England 1830–1914* (Manchester: Manchester University Press, 2013).
5. H.C. Sarkar, ed., *Life and Letters of Raja Rammohun Roy by Sophia Dobson Collet* (Calcutta: A.C. Sarkar at the B.M. Press, 1913). This edition also incorporated material from the work of another leader English Unitarian woman supporter of the Brahmo Samaj, *Mary Carpenter's Last Days in England of the Rajuh Rammohun Roy* (London, 1866).
6. M. Sinha, *Colonial Masculinity. The 'manly Englishman' and the 'effeminate Bengali' in the Late Nineteenth Century* (Manchester: Manchester University Press, 1995), p. 2.
7. Kris Manjapra, 'Introduction', in S. Bose and K. Manjapra, eds., *Cosmopolitan Thought Zones: South Asia and the Global Circulation of Ideas* (2010), p. 1.
8. For simplicity, I will in future refer to this complex network as the Brahmo-Unitarian connection.
9. Letter from Lucy Aikin to William Ellery Channing Sept 6, 1831, printed in *Memoirs, Miscellanies and Letters of the Late Lucy Aikin*, ed. P.H. Le Breton (London: Longman & Co., 1864), p. 230 (italics in original). Sarkar quotes Aikin's letter in his Introduction (p. lxxiv) to his 1913 edition of *Collet's Life and Letters.*
10. For discussion of missionary imperialism see, for example: S. Thorne, 'Missionary-Imperial Feminism', in M.T. Huber and N.C. Lutkehaus, eds., *Gendered Missions. Women and Men in Missionary Discourse and Practice* (Ann Arbor: University of Michigan Press, 199). pp. 39–66.
11. Leela Gandhi, *Affective Communities: Anticolonial Thought, fin-de-siècle Radicalism, and the Politics of Friendship* (Durham, NC: Duke University Press, 2006), p. 10.
12. P. Cheah and B. Robbins, eds., *Cosmopolitics: Thinking and Feeling Beyond the Nation* (Minneapolis: University of Minnesota Press, 1998).

13. See Sinha, *Colonial Masculinity.*
14. Keshub Chunder Sen, 'My Impressions of England', in Writers Workshop, ed. *Keshub Chunder Sen in England: Diaries, Sermons, Addresses and Epistles* (Calcutta, 1980), p. 460.
15. *Bamabodhini Patrika*, no. 353 (June 1894).
16. H.C. Sarkar, 'Sophia Dobson Collet, a Biographical Sketch', in Sarkar, ed., *Life and Letters of Raja Rammohun Roy*, p. xxxii. Sarkar hoped to go on to write a full free-standing biography of Collet, but this project was never completed.
17. Kathryn Gleadle, 'Collet, Sophia Dobson (1822–1894)', *Oxford Dictionary of National Biography* (Oxford University Press, 2004) [http://www.oxforddnb.com/view/article/41272, accessed Oct 11, 2016].
18. Sarkar, 'Sophia Dobson Collet', p. xxxi.
19. Collet, ed., *The Life and Letters*, pp. 163–164; W.J. Fox, *A Discourse on Occasion of the Death of Rajah Rammohun Roy* (London, 1833).
20. Sarkar, 'Sophia Dobson Collet', p. x.
21. Her detailed notes of Fox's sermons of 1841–45 are quoted in R. Garnett and E. Garnett, *The Life of W.J. Fox, Public Teacher and Social Reformer 1786–1864.* (London and New York: John Lane, 1910), pp. 223–229.
22. See Gleadle, *The Early Feminists* p. 18 for the influence of American Transcendentalists on English Unitarians. While some of those influenced by Transcendentalism moved beyond the Christian Unitarian fold, others remained within it.
23. Moncure D. Conway, *Autobiography: Memories and Experiences*, Vol. 2 (London: Cassell & Co., 1904), p. 39; T. F. Wright, ed., *The Cosmopolitan Lyceum. Lecture Culture and the Globe in Nineteenth-Century America* (Amherst and Boston: University of Massachusetts Press, 2013).
24. Schwartz, *Infidel Feminism*, pp. 57–58.
25. Letter from S.D. Collet to her aunt Mary (undated), Collet Papers, ref: 7CCF/survey/12.2.4. See also letter from theist F.W. Newman to S.D. Collet, July 26, 1849 on his opposition to pantheism. Collet's friend Sara Hennell, another former Unitarian, also identified herself publicly as a pantheist at this time. See Schwarz *Infidel Feminism*, pp. 56, 115–116.
26. S.D. Collet, 'An Intellectual Diary' (1857), hand-written diary, entry for March 16th, Collet Papers, ref: 7CCF/12.2.7.
27. Ibid.
28. Letter from S.D. Collet to M. Estlin, Oct 5, 1885, Collet Papers, ref: 7CCF/11.3.
29. Conway, *Autobiography: Memories and Experiences*, Vol. 2, p. 39; Gleadle, 'Collet, Sophia Dobson'.

30. See Gleadle, *The First Feminists*, p. 59 for the close links between Unitarianism and Broad Church Anglicanism at this time.
31. Letters from F.P. Cobbe to S.D. Collet, March 1 1861 and April 11 1861, Collet Papers, ref: 7CCF/11.7; letters from F.W. Newman to S.D. Collet, Feb 7 1863, March 2, 1863, July 3, 1864, Dec 7, 1867, Collet Papers, ref: 7CCF/survey/12.2.6.
32. *Bamabodhini Patrika*, 5:72 (Aug–Sept 1869), pp. 76–77.
33. 'Bilatiyo Shongbad' [News from England], *Bamabodhini Patrika*,6, 87, (Oct–Nov1870), pp. 210–211.
34. C. Hall, 'Missionary Stories: Gender and Ethnicity in England in the 1830s and 1840s', in C. Hall, ed., *White Male and Middle Class. Explorations of Feminism and History* (Cambridge: Polity Press, 1992), pp. 205–254.
35. Letter from S.D. Collet to M. Estlin, April 7, 1886, Collet Papers, ref: 7CCF/11.3.
36. Ibid.
37. Collet, 'An Intellectual Diary', March 5th, 1857.
38. Ibid. Aug.12th, 1857.
39. Sarkar, 'Sophia Dobson Collet', p. xv.
40. Letter from Keshub Chunder Sen to S.D. Collet, 18 Dec 1874, Collet Papers, ref: 7CCF/11.5.
41. 'Bilatiyo Shongbad' [News from England], pp. 210–211.
42. Sarkar, 'Sophia Dobson Collet', p. xxxii.
43. ibid. p. xxxii.
44. Clare Midgley, 'Indian feminist Pandita Ramabai and Transnational Liberal Religious Networks in the Nineteenth-Century World', in Clare Midgley, Alison Twells and Julie Carlier, eds., *Women in Transnational History: Connecting the Local and the Global* (London: Routledge, 2016), pp. 13–33.
45. Sophia Dobson Collet, *George Jacob Holyoake and Modern Atheism. A Biographical and Critical Essay* (London: Trübner & Co, 1855), p. 42.
46. Sophia Dobson Collet, *Indian Theism and its Relation to Christianity* (London: Strahan & Co., 1870).
47. ibid., p.29.
48. Ibid., p. 31.
49. Sophia Dobson Collet, *An Historical Sketch of the Brahmo Samaj* (2nd ed., Calcutta: Navavidhan Publication Committee, 1940) [reproduction of original 1st ed., Calcutta: Calcutta Central Press Company, 1873)],Preface, p. ii.
50. Ibid., p.46.
51. S.D. Collet, ed., *Keshub Chunder Sen's English Visit* (London: Strahan & Co., 1871).

52. S.D. Collet, ed., *The Brahmo Year-Book for 1876* (London and Edinburgh: Williams and Norgate, 1876), Preface, p. 8.
53. S.D. Collet, ed., *The Brahmo Year- Book for 1877* (London and Edinburgh: Williams and Norgate, 1877), Preface, pp. 5, 6.
54. Letter from W.H. Channing to S.D. Collet, Feb 27, 1877, Collet Papers, ref: 7CCF/survey/12.2.4.
55. S.D. Collet, ed., *The Brahmo Year-Book for 1881* (London and Edinburgh: Williams and Norgate, 1882), pp. 139–140.
56. S.D. Collet, ed., *The Brahmo Year-Book for 1881* p.25.
57. S.D. Collet, ed., *The Brahmo Year-Book for 1882* (London and Edinburgh: Williams and Norgate, 1883), pp. 81–84.
58. Eventually published as S. Sastri, *History of the Brahmo Samaj*, 2 vols. (Calcutta: Sadharan Brahmo Samaj, 1911, 1912) it drew on Collet's own publications. See opening of Preface to Vol. 1 for acknowledgement of Collet's role in urging Sastri to write the book.
59. Nagendar Nath Chatterji, *Mahatma Raja Rammohan Rayer Jibancharita* [Life of the illustrious Raja Ram Mohan Roy] (Calcutta: Roy Press, 1881); review of book by S.D. Collet in Collet, ed., *The Brahmo Year-Book for 1882*, p. 74.
60. Sarkar, 'Sophia Dobson Collet', p. xxx.
61. Collet, *The Life and Letters*, p. 165.
62. Ibid. pp. 3, 7, 10. It is important to exercise caution in using the text of the published biography as a whole as a source for understanding Collet's perspectives on Roy's religious beliefs. Only the first quarter of the published work is in her own words. My discussion here focuses on the parts of the book written by Collet herself.
63. Ibid., pp. 17–18, 23.
64. *Reasoner*, 4:91 (1848), pp. 175–176; Collet, *George Jacob Holyoake*, pp. 42–43, as discussed in Schwartz, *Infidel Feminism*, p. 58; see also pp. 116–117.
65. Collet, *The Life and Letters*, p. 33.
66. Collet, ed., *The Brahmo Year-Book for 1876*, pp. 48–49.
67. Her letter was published in *Bamabodhini Patrika*, 9, 124, Nov–Dec 1873, pp. 258–260 with a note introducing Collet to its readers as a leading English supporter of the Brahmo Samaj, and praising her efforts to learn Bengali.
68. Clare Midgley, 'Liberal Religion and the 'Woman Question' between East and West: Perspectives from a Nineteenth-Century Bengali Women's Journal', *Gender & History*, 25, 3 (2013), pp. 443–458.
69. *Brahmo Marriages. Their Past History and Present Position* (London: Strachan & Co, 1871). I have been unable to track down a copy of this pamphlet.
70. Collet, ed., *The Brahmo Year-Book for 1878*, pp. 15, 17.

71. Ibid., p. 18.
72. S.D, Collet, ed., *The Brahmo Year-Book for 1880* (London and Edinburgh: Williams and Norgate, 1880), p. 19.
73. Letters from S.D. Collet to M. Estlin, Dec 21, 1885; Dec 31, 1885; Jan 6, 1886, April 27, 1886, Aug 31, 1885; 6th Sept 1885; 7th Sept 1885; 12 Sept 1885; 19 Sept. 1885; 1 Dec. 1885; Dec 12, 1885, Jan 7, 1886, Jan 19, 1886, Feb 14, 1887, Aug 16, 1887, Collet Papers, ref: 7CCF/11.3.
74. Ibid., Sept 7, 1885.
75. John Stevens, 'Marriage, Duty and Civilization: Keshab Chandra Sen and the Cuch Bihar Controversy in Metropolitan and Colonial Context', *South Asian History and Culture* (2016) DOI: 10.1080/19472498.2016.1223720.
76. Elleke Boehmer, *Empire, the National, and the Postcolonial 1890–1920. Resistance in Interaction* (Oxford: Oxford University Press, 2002), p. 17.

CHAPTER 3

Henry Polak: The Cosmopolitan Life of a Jewish Theosophist, Friend of India and Anti-racist Campaigner

Abstract Henry Polak (1882–1959), a British-born lawyer, journalist and editor of *Indian Opinion*, campaigned with Mohandas Gandhi against restrictions on South African Indians and against the indentured labour system. Founder of the Indian Overseas Association in 1920, he worked with Indians across the diaspora against racism and discriminations. Most in tune with Indian political liberals, he worked with them for Indian independence. His life of border-crossings and his affective cosmopolitanism were inspired by his spiritual cosmopolitanism. His reading across cosmopolitan thought zones saw his embrace of Theosophy and universal equality. He drew strong links between Theosophical beliefs and the Universal Declaration of Human Rights.

Keywords Spiritual cosmopolitanism · Affective cosmopolitanism · H.S.L. Polak · Indian Overseas Association · Cosmopolitan thought zones · Theosophy

Henry Polak (1882–1959), a British-born lawyer, journalist and activist, campaigned on behalf of Indians across the British Empire against racism and discriminations, in the first half of the twentieth century.[1] Beginning with an intimate friendship and collaboration with Mohandas Gandhi in South Africa and in India during the years 1903–1916, Polak built a life of 'innovative border-crossings'.[2] His career spanned the period from the

J. Haggis et al., *Cosmopolitan Lives on the Cusp of Empire*,
DOI 10.1007/978-3-319-52748-2_3

struggle against the erection of the 'Great White Walls' around settler colonies in the pre-World War 1 years, through the strengthening of anti-colonial movements in the 1920s and 1930s, to the Universal Declaration of Human Rights and beyond.[3] He died in 1959, still involved with anti-racist struggles, now against apartheid.

From his youth Polak read religious texts from a number of different traditions, which laid the basis of his spiritual cosmopolitanism, belief in human equality and the necessity of comity. During his life he built friendships and collegial relationships with many Indians, in the sub-continent and across the diaspora. His spiritual cosmopolitanism and his affective cosmopolitanism were productive in practical terms. They nourished his political activism and sustained his commitment to work for legislative change.

This chapter begins by examining the personal, social forces and ethical imperatives, which led him to move beyond British society, culture and Judeo-Christian traditions to involve himself deeply in the struggle of others. The chapter discusses the rich and complex nature of his career and achievements and explores the role of friendship, and the written word in his activism and cosmopolitanism. Finally, it raises questions about the limits to his cosmopolitanism.

What Ethical Imperatives?

Leela Gandhi has posed the question, 'what ethical imperatives… rendered some Europeans immune to the ubiquitous temptations of… empire.… to betray the claims of possessive nationalism in favor of solidarity with foreigners, outsiders, alleged inferiors?'[4] For Polak, the source of these imperatives lay in his youth in late nineteenth-century London. Born into a commercial family in London's Jewish community and without the benefit of a university education, Polak might seem a most unlikely figure to develop a broad understanding of comparative religions, to devote himself to colonised peoples oppressed by his own nation and to choose to stand with them against his own fellow citizens.

Paul Gilroy's comment that the 'methodical cultivation of a degree of estrangement from one's own culture and history… might qualify as essential to a cosmopolitan commitment',[5] appears crucial to Polak's cosmopolitanism. Polak details a number of influences contributing to 'a degree of estrangement' from his own background, which made it possible for him to relate to others on a more equal basis. As a young person, rather than acquiring a fixed and unchanging notion of British-ness and any conviction of British uniqueness, he was acutely aware of the variety and diversity among its peoples. He credits a teacher's emphasis upon the diverse origins of the British people, including

> Celtic, (possibly) Phoenician, Roman…Angle, Saxon, Jute, Norman, Scandinavian, Iberian, Dutch, French (Huguenot, Jewish, German, Polish, Italian, and even African, Indian and Chinese elements had all helped to enrich the national (not to speak of the imperial) inheritance and upon their absorption, had made up the British people as we know them to-day.[6]

His own family history spoke to this, as his Jewish forebears had come from Holland about a hundred years before his birth, while earlier generations of the family came from Poland and Germany.[7] Proud of both his 'English and foreign descent', he seemed to comfortably embrace people across their world and was able to enter into their concerns and interests (Fig. 3.1).

> Insularity was to me never very comprehensible. I was as much 'at home', so to speak, 'abroad', as I was in the land of my birth.[8]

He grew to adulthood at the height of empire, in an era swamped by imperial ideology. As Schneer notes, 'The Imperial drumbeat was steady and all-enveloping in turn-of-the-century London'.[9] Yet Polak managed to develop a critical stance towards this drumbeat, influenced by his father's work as an advertising agent for a pro-Boer newspaper along with his experience of reading continental newspapers that shocked him initially with their 'anti British tone', but which made him understand the political nature of accounts of current events.[10]

Robert Gregory attributes Polak's ability to commit himself to the Indian cause to 'his awareness of the persecution suffered by minority groups', including Jews.[11] This is only partly true. In fact, Polak was not deeply engaged with Judaism, and could be quite critical of Jewish people, having a 'degree of estrangement' from the faith of his ancestors. On his death, the London *Jewish Chronicle* noted that he played 'little part in Jewish activities'.[12] Polak's complicated relationship with Judaism, both in the London of his youth and in South Africa in early adulthood helped to foster his cosmopolitanism and anti-racism. In his formative years, he knew of the persecution that Jews had experienced throughout history and contemporaneously in the pogroms of Eastern and Central Europe, as

Fig. 3.1 Portrait of H. S. L. Polak

Source: Golden number of *Indian Opinion* 1914: Souvenir of the passive resistance movement in South Africa, 1906–1914, Courtesy Professor Uma Dhupelia-Mesthrie

well as discrimination in London's East End.[13] He credits his 'youthful agnosticism' to his 'dislike of the ceremonial'. His parents were moving away from orthodoxy and he did not learn a lot about Jewish religion. He felt 'drawn outwards towards a larger life of spiritual experience'.[14] He was also aware of the hierarchy and prejudice which Sephardic families like his felt towards the Ashkenazy Jews.[15]

> Even as a child, I was made aware of two main currents of human experience – the tendency to segregation, separateness, and differentiation, upon a basis of relative superiority and inferiority on one hand; and that towards interdependence, intermingling, and unification, upon a basis of mutual compatibility, on the other.[16]

His South African sojourn also made him aware how oppressed and marginalised groups could also attempt to improve their own situation by supporting discrimination against other groups. He critiqued South African Jews, who joined in discrimination against Indians. Commenting in 1911 upon Durban's Jewish mayor's banning of Indians from the city's coronation celebrations he wrote,

> Unfortunately, many of our co-religionists in South Africa appear never to have learnt this fore-most lesson of the age long persecution of the Jewish people, for in spite of the complete freedom and liberty with which they are vested, so soon as they set foot upon South African soil, they do not hesitate to join in the hue and cry against the disinherited residents of the sub-continent.[17]

Polak gained a studentship at the London School of Economics, but was there only briefly, as his father could not afford to keep him there. He did spend a year in Switzerland at a commercial college, but back in London, working as an insurance clerk, he sought out educational opportunities as an evening student and at public lectures. He studied commerce and languages at Queen's Road commercial evening school, where he met Millie Graham Downs, his future wife. She was 'an ardent social reformer' introducing him to the 'wide lecture program at Southgate Road Brotherhood Church under the Reverend Bruce Wallace'. The politics of this congregation was 'Christian socialist and pacifist... there was a strong Tolstoyan anarchist current' and a number of Quakers were members.[18] Reading and discussing Tolstoy influenced his social habits; he gave up alcohol and tobacco and became a vegetarian.[19] He heard the Theosophist Annie Besant lecture and although impressed, did not embrace Theosophy at that stage.

Millie and Polak also attended lectures and concerts at the South Place Ethical Society, an important and long-standing Freethinking community, where Collet, at an earlier incarnation of this congregation, had heard Roy speak. Polak took to heart the motto on its lecture platform – 'to thine own self be true'. Millie's gift of a ring inscribed with this motto, when he departed for South Africa, is expressive of the intertwining of the bond between them and their ethical commitment to humanity. His understanding of his 'own self' as 'a spark from an emanation of the Universal self' gives a clue to his respect for others, and to his religious cosmopolitanism.[20]

Clearly, even before he went to South Africa, he was seeking new ideas and reading widely, including the anarchist Kropotkin's *Fields, Factories and Workshops;* Tolstoy, initially for his 'social and political teaching' but 'later for his spiritual guidance' which 'drew [me] out of my superficial agnosticism'; and more widely, religious classics from outside Europe: Romesh Chandrasekhar Dutt's verse summaries of the great Sanskrit epics, the *Mahabharata* and the *Ramayana,* as well as Edwin Arnold's verse rendering of the *Bhagavad Gita*[21] and Buddhist scripture such as *Dhammapada* and Edwin Arnold's interpretation *Light of Asia.*[22] Polak commented:

> These books helped me to sense that there was a whole world of philosophy and religious experience beyond my ken.[23]

In South Africa, he became a life-long Theosophist, a belief system, which rejected 'social barriers based upon race, sex or creed'[24] and held that all faiths contributed to humanity. This contrasted with imperial Christianity's shibboleth that the only road to salvation was via conversion to Christianity. His commitment to the brotherhood and, indeed, the sisterhood of humanity rested on what he saw as timeless truths drawn from many religious traditions, which guided his actions. These beliefs combined with his legal training and what he termed a sense of British fair play: this last rather curious, given his long opposition to British imperialism. Even when he was arrested in 1913, for supporting the Indian Passive Resistance, he later recalled:

> In view of the fact that I, as an outsider, had so often counselled Indian passive resisters to challenge arrest, I felt that it would be highly dishonourable for me – an Englishman – to draw back before such a risk, and I did not hesitate to join them.[25]

He held to these beliefs of equality and brotherhood all his life, although the challenge of Nazism led him to reconsider his pacifism. When writing to Gandhi late in 1939 about Gandhi's opposition to Indian participation in World War Two, he drew upon Hinduism, invoking 'the deepest and holiest sense of duty such as Sri Krishna spoke of to Arjuna' to destroy the Nazi 'locust regime'.[26] He referred to Krishna's teaching of the morality of a 'lawful war'.[27]

The basis of his anti-racism and cosmopolitanism was derived from his views about religion,

> All the great religious teachers and spiritual guides have taught from time immemorial that mankind is one and indivisible, that all men, of whatever race and colour are the embodiment of a fragment of the one Divine life and are therefore brothers.[28]

Deeply interested in inter-religionist movements, in 'world fellowship and the world citizenship movement', he attended the World Congress of Religions in 1937 in Geneva.[29]

His decades of struggle against racial hierarchies saw his participation in a conference of Non-Government Organisations to consider the draft Universal Declaration of Human Rights in Geneva in 1948. In 1953 he gave evidence to the United Nations Commission on Racial Discrimination in South Africa.[30] Addressing the Theosophical Society at its headquarters in Adyar, India, in 1956, he made a direct connection between Theosophy and the Universal Declaration of Human Rights, noting that the first object of Theosophy to proceed 'without distinction of race, creed, sex, caste or colour' had been substantially incorporated into the UN Declaration.[31]

Consorting with Indians

Polak went to South Africa in 1903, when he was 21 years on a family-sponsored business venture, inspired at least in part, by the hope this separation would diminish his attachment to Millie, a gentile. In South Africa, he was struck by the diversity of the population:

> People known contemptuously as 'Kaffirs', white people of various nationalities, the small Indian community, and people referred to as 'coloureds'.[32]

Most of the Indians had been brought to the colony as indentured labourers under a British-devised scheme, which met the labour needs of plantations after the abolition of slavery.[33] A smaller number, 'passenger Indians', had come on their own volition as merchants or as small businessmen. There were very few Indian professionals such as Gandhi, a lawyer. The vast majority of the population were Africans. The white settlers, Boer and English, former enemies, had speedily joined together, after the Boer war, in a pact of whiteness, determined to exclude Indians, the few resident Chinese, and Africans, from social and political citizenship.[34] This environment symbolised the poles around 'race' to be traversed during the twentieth century.[35] There was the possibility of mutual co-operation and learning across historical and cultural differences and, on the other hand, a path to separation, segregation, domination and violence. Thus, South Africa was a crucial place to reach out in fraternity and to emphasise the common humanity of mankind.

Polak met Gandhi in a vegetarian restaurant in Johannesburg in 1904. Polak, the then sub-editor of the *Transvaal Critic,* was quite 'knowledgeable of the many inequalities suffered by the Indian community'.[36] Indeed, Polak wanted to meet Gandhi, having 'watched a verbal duel, in an evening paper, between him and the Medical Officer of Health in Johannesburg, as to whose was the responsibility for the outbreak of plague in the Indian location'.[37] They shared interests in vegetarianism, Tolstoy and a recent book by Adolf Just, *Return to Nature.* At this meeting, Polak introduced Gandhi to Ruskin's, *Unto This Last,* a volume which Gandhi felt reflected some of 'his deepest convictions' and made him transform his own life.[38] The mutual attraction was intense. Gandhi later wrote,

> Mr Polak's candour drew me to him... We seemed to hold closely similar views on the essential things of life. He liked simple life.[39]

Gandhi commented, 'I judged Polak within five hours... I at once saw what he was, and since then he became my man', his 'soulmate and lieutenant'.[40] Gandhi soon asked him to join *Indian Opinion,* the newspaper of the British Indian Association in South Africa, and the agitation against discriminatory legislation. These were the heady days of the struggle of South African Indians to gain the rights of British subjects. Polak left the *Transvaal Critic*, where he felt constrained in his political expression, becoming the editor of *Indian Opinion* from 1905 to 1916.

Polak's relationship with Gandhi was unusual and daring for the period, alienating him from the South African Jewish community, who saw him as 'consorting with Indians'.[41] Gandhi notes, 'we began to live as blood brothers',[42] in Gandhi's family home. Gandhi even worked to bring Polak and Millie together by intervening on their behalf to Polak's father. The closeness of the relationship between the two men saw Gandhi act as Polak's best man. Proceedings were temporarily halted when the Chief Magistrate thought the marriage was between an Indian and a white woman, illegal in the Transvaal. After assurances from Gandhi that Polak 'in spite of appearances, physical, political and social…was in fact, a "White man"' the ceremony proceeded.[43] It had no religious elements, as Gandhi commented, 'Their common religion was the religion of ethics.'[44] Later, the couple lived in the Phoenix Settlement, Gandhi's first ashram.

Polak was closely involved with Gandhi during the years 1907–1914 in the Indian Passive Resistance Struggle against the compulsory registration of Indians and Chinese by the Transvaal authorities.[45] Under Gandhi counsel, most refused to register and 'by the end of January 2008, 2000 Indians and Chinese had been imprisoned'.[46] Some were flogged or had their property auctioned to pay fines, while others were deported. Indians and Chinese also protested against the Immigration Restriction Act and other punitive and discriminatory policies. Gandhi honed his method of *Satyagraha* (non-violent resistance), involving the refusal to obey unjust laws with the intention of appealing to the humanity of the oppressors and to the sympathy of the general public to force change. Mesthrie notes:

> *Indian Opinion* played a very significant role throughout the course of the passive resistance struggle. At one level it highlighted the major issues, chronicled the activities of the resisters and brought Indian grievances to the notice of influential people on Britain and India. At another level it became an active agent in mobilizing and organizing resistance.[47]

Polak, very much Gandhi's lieutenant,[48] was from 1906 assistant secretary of the British Indian Association (BIA), formed to advance the interests of Indians.[49]

On Gandhi's suggestion Polak began studying law, becoming articled to Gandhi in 1905. Gandhi wanted a legal assistant believing it would also aid the work of the struggle and of *Indian Opinion*.[50] In the racially divided South Africa of the time, it was remarkable for a white man to study law under an Indian. Once qualified, in 1908, Polak defended the passive resisters in court and took over Gandhi's practice.

Cosmopolitan Thought Zones

The close friendship and collaboration of Gandhi and Polak was based upon reading, and conversations between 'different cultural, linguistic and political communities in the pursuit of shared goals'.[51] Gandhi introduced

Polak to Max Muller's *India: What can it teach us?*, an account of India's rich philosophical and religious culture, which led its readers to think critically about Western dominance. Polak introduced Gandhi to Thomas à Kempis. Both were interested in different religious communities and their sacred writings. Millie Polak recalled:

> When guests were present, philosophies of different countries would be compared and many varieties of religious and mystic experiences dwelt upon. One never-failing theme was the different customs of East and West, and the different outlook upon life that various races of the world exemplified.[52]

Polak deepened his understanding of Hinduism:

> I studied the great Hindu scripture, *Bhagavad Gita* with Gandhiji in 1905, while living with his family in Johannesburg. The teaching of Lord Krishna to his pupil and devotee, Prince Arjuna was always deep in his consciousness. 'By whatever path men approach Me, even so I do welcome them; for the path men take from every side is Mine.' That teaching had a deep impression on me and helped me decide, unwilling at first, but upon Gandhiji's' persuasion to become a member of the Theosophical Society and to join the Johannesburg lodge.[53]

The *Indian Opinion* was produced in a number of different languages[54] aimed at the diverse Indian communities in South Africa and British and Indian supporters of their struggle.[55] As editor and frequent writer in its columns, Polak was a crucial participant in what Hofmeyr terms 'one of the great intellectual archives of the world'.[56] It was created in a cosmopolitan thought zone as Hofmeyr details,

> Produced in a context of multiple diasporic intersections in southern Africa, the paper's pages are woven from a variety of global intellectual filaments, drawn from larger trajectories of migration. These intellectual maps included the imperial and subimperial triangle of Africa-India-Britain; the dispersal of indentured Indian workers (Mauritius, Fiji, Caribbean, Burma, Ceylon, Malaya); the flashpoints where voluntary Indian migration encountered the global color line (British Columbia, the United States, Australia, New Zealand); the sacred geographies of Islam and Hinduism, followed by Zoroastrianism, Jainism and Christianity; circuits of back internationalism (Universal Races Congress, Booker T. Washington, W.E.B. Du Bois); and

> configurations within and between other European empires (Portuguese, French, German).[57]

Readers were encouraged to read across many traditions, including Gujarati titles, works in English by Tolstoy, Ruskin, Emerson, Mazzini, ethical, religious and theological works.[58] Extracts from and references to Polak and Gandhi's own wide reading were found in its pages. Indeed, Polak refers to Thoreau's pamphlet, *On the Duty of Civil Disobedience*, which Gandhi urged him to publish 'as a supplement to *Indian Opinion*'.[59] Polak and Gandhi also explored the notion of 'race' in its pages, with Polak publishing a pamphlet critiquing the ideas of Johannesburg journalist L.E. Neame, on 'The Asiatic Danger' to white supremacy in the colonies. Polak interrogated white racism as a 'symptom of Western industrial capitalism'.[60] It was most likely Polak who, under a pseudonym, reviewed Jean Finot, *Racial Prejudice* in 1907. This text influenced Gandhi, accelerating

> his transformation in South Africa from one who was seeking equality with Europeans to one who spoke in terms of equality for all.[61]

An Envoy for the Indians, Building Networks Across India

On a number of occasions from 1909, Gandhi and the BIA sent Polak on a speaking tour to India to inform and gain the support of the Indian public about the South African situation and to gather funds for Passive Resisters. On these visits, he represented the South African Indians at the INC, as well as those in East Africa and Zanzibar. In 1909, he spoke to many groups across the country, also visiting Ceylon to arrange the repatriation of 67 South African Indians who had been deported for participating in the resistance.[62] During these visits, Polak made many Indian friends including the liberal South Indian publisher, G.A. Natesan, editor of the Madras based, *Indian Review*, and began writing for this and many other Indian publications, circulating information about the South African struggle and India's position within the British Empire. Natesan published two books by Polak in 1909, *The Indians of South Africa; helots within the empire and how they are treated*[63] and also *A tragedy of empire: the treatment of British Indians in the Transvaal; an appeal to India*.[64] Both were intended to inform Indian public opinion about the Indian situation in South Africa. Polak gathered £6,000 to further the work of the BIA.[65] He became a prolific public speaker, broadcaster and writer on Indian matters, on internationalism and the scourge of racism and published widely in Indian, British and American publications.

As part of a BIA delegation, Polak also attended the Universal Races Congress in London, in 1911. This unusual assembly of missionaries, anthropologists, anti-colonial activists, intellectuals and assorted others, aimed

> to discuss in the light of modern knowledge and the modern conscience, the general relations subsisting between peoples of the West and those of the East, between so-called white and so-called coloured peoples, with a view to encouraging between them fuller understanding, the most friendly feelings and a heartier cooperation.[66]

This was a crucial moment for the airing of anticolonial cosmopolitanisms,[67] and both exposed and facilitated networks of connection among the 'globally oriented elite' of African, African-American and Asian professionals, intellectuals and political activists'.[68] Polak spoke about the South African Indian campaign for justice.[69] He was also deputed by the Transvaal Chinese Association 'to represent their grievances to the Chinese Consul-General' in London.[70] Back in South Africa, Polak was arrested in 1913 while supporting the Indian opposition to the poll tax imposed upon them. He refused to apply for bail or pay fines, which would have seen him released in solidarity with the Indians and served a 3-month sentence.[71]

Gandhi left India in 1914. They had agreed that the Polaks would also return to London when the South African campaign came to an end, so that their children could be 'brought up in an atmosphere free from racial and colour prejudice'.[72] However, Gandhi asked Polak to stay behind to oversee the implementation of the Smuts-Gandhi agreement, a somewhat unsatisfactory compromise agreement with the South African government, aimed to settle the Indians' concerns.[73]

On his return trip to England, Polak made a long detour to India in 1916–1917 to speak on the evils of the indenture system, on South African Indian problems and to confer with Gandhi. As a BIA delegate he again addressed the INC and various other gatherings, including The Servants of India society in Bombay, founded by Gandhi's mentor, social reformer and nationalist G.K. Gokhale (1866–1915). He spoke to the members of the Vizagapatam District Association on indentured labour and to the Home Rule League at Cocanda. He spoke in smaller centres such as Gooty and to the Ahmedabad Students Brotherhood, while the District Congress Committee of Ajmer, planning a great demonstration against indentured labour, invited him to address them.[74]

Throughout his Indian travels, Polak was under surveillance by British intelligence. At times it was difficult to arrange public meetings due to the blocks placed by British officials.[75] Police questioned his hosts, and undercover British representatives attended his talks.[76] Addressing a meeting in Allahabad critiquing the superior position of the white settler dominions within the British Empire in May 1917, he joked about the fact that the Criminal Investigation Department would have a spy in the meeting, ready to report back. He asserted that no public meeting in India was complete without

> The cordial cooperation of those kindly guardians of the public conscience, those simple, selfless unassuming souls, the gentlemen of the Criminal Investigation Department.[77]

By 1917 and his return to London, the campaign against indenture was achieving some success. Polak was

> One of a small group responsible for the termination of indenture labour to Natal (1911), Closing of recruitment of indentured labour throughout the Empire (1917) and abolition of indenture (1920).[78]

The small group was diverse, bringing together activists from different backgrounds, including Gandhi; G.K. Gokhale; Totaram Sanadhya (1876–1947), a former indentured worker; the nationalist journalist Banarsidas Chaturvedi (1892–1925); and C. F. Andrews (1871–1940), the Anglican priest and missionary who worked closely with Gandhi. Polak's return to London marked the end of his South African residence, but he always maintained an active interest in South African affairs and wrote extensively about them.[79]

While the South African interlude has been represented as crucial to Gandhi's political development,[80] Gandhi and Polak's joint activities and discussions were transformative for both of them. Gandhi's relationship with

Henry Polak in South Africa enabled Gandhi to move from a life as a middle-class lawyer 'in the direction of a more simplified life of public service'.[81] In South Africa, Polak found Theosophy, which confirmed his worldview; and discovered his life's work in combatting racism and working on a global stage, in particular for Indian equality. In these years, Polak became an experienced political activist, a lawyer, an accomplished public speaker, writer, and editor. His friendships and working relationships across 'racial', and cultural boundaries were remarkable for the period. He had become an international figure, particularly in the sub-continent and South Africa.

Friendships and Collaborations

Polak entered into friendly and collegial relationships with a number of Indian leaders, Gandhi being only the first. His 'affective cosmopolitanism' saw these relationships maintained over decades. He positioned himself as learning from these men, as a 'friend alongside' rather than being a commanding white man.

> Many of my closest Indian friends have been older than myself... I have learnt (or tried to learn) so much from their more mature experience.[82]

Indeed, Gandhi advised him on the eve of his first Indian visit 'to place himself unreservedly under [Gokhale's] instructions'.[83]

Unlike Collett, he could share domestic and familial spaces. But sensitive to Brahminic customs, he noted later that when he met Natesan,

> In those days, hospitality to an Englishman in a Brahmin home was somewhat difficult; so Natesan arranged for my accommodation, as his guest, first at the Y.M.C.A., and later at a nearby hotel,[84]

continuing,

> On a later visit to Madras I had the privilege of enjoying the hospitality of Mr and Mrs Natesan, and so learnt something of the beauty of family life in South India.[85]

Later, he hosted Natesan and many other Indians, including Gandhi, in his London home.[86] Polak and Gandhi always maintained a mutual interest in each other's family. In London in 1909, Gandhi was a frequent guest at the home of Polak's parents. Polak's father, J. H. Polak, became an enthusiastic member of the British support committee of the BIA.[87] Polak's sister, Maud, also worked with Gandhi and the BIA.[88] As the correspondence between Gandhi and Polak diminished in the later 1920s, 1930s and 1940s, Gandhi still enquired about Polak's parents, Millie, their children and extended family.[89]

Gandhi used Polak as an entry point into London and British connections, for a number of Indians visitors, thus advising G.K. Devadhar, a foundation member of the Servants of India Society and promoter of women's and basic education,

> Of course, Polak will be your guide, friend and philosopher. He will take you to all Englishmen I know politically.[90]

Strains in the Polak-Gandhi Friendship

Despite their closeness, Polak's relationship with Gandhi was not that of an 'uncritical disciple'.[91] They disagreed over a number of things, including Gandhi's support for the British war effort in World War One. Polak saw it as inconsistent with Gandhi's non-violent beliefs, his 'profession of *ahimsa*'.[92] Concerned about the rise of communalism, Polak feared that Muslims were being marginalised by the INC.[93] He preferred more conventional approaches to resistance, believing that Gandhi's non-cooperation movement would easily descend into violence. When this more radical faction gained control of the INC in 1919, Polak felt unable to 'conscientiously adopt or advocate that policy'.[94] Gandhi went on to lead the Congress from 1920 and Polak surrendered his position of editor of *India*, the publication of the INC London committee. Despite their divergence, until the 1940s, they maintained a friendly, but sometimes fiercely critical, correspondence and fondly remembered their days of collaboration in South Africa. In 1930, Gandhi wrote to Polak, when the INC had declared Indian independence of Britain, 'If you had lived here as I have during the past 15 years, you would have done what I have' continuing, 'Anyway our love will stand the strain of any difference in views and actions'.[95] In 1939 Polak wrote:

> It must have been in our karma that this close link between us, which has remained unbroken for so long, should have been forged.[96]

However, the Second World War posed challenges to thinking 'beyond the nation'. Polak was critical of Gandhi's failure to recognise the great danger posed by Nazism. Gandhi believed Polak was criticising him during a North American lecture tour, confiding to mutual friend, Agatha Harrison, 'Everybody I have met is sore at heart about his doings in U.S.A.' but continued, 'please give my love to Henry and Millie'.[97]

Although they disagreed in these last years, Polak had sought to explicate Gandhi and Indian views to the world. In 1910, he contributed a biographical sketch on Gandhi to an edition of his speeches and writings[98]; indeed he and his wife, Millie, were said to be 'about the first in the West to interpret Gandhiji's message'.[99] Millie's 1931 book, *Gandhi: The Man* sought to give a human picture of Gandhi. After Gandhi's death, Polak was a co-author of *Mahatma Gandhi: the father of modern India* (1949). In 1956, he was invited to India to assist with the collection and preservation of Gandhi's voluminous archive, identifying what Gandhi had written in early columns of *Indian Opinion.*[100] A perusal of the 98 volumes of Gandhi's collected works show that many original letters and other works were donated by Polak, enabling a fuller understanding of Gandhi's life and work for posterity.

'He struggled to promote the rights of Indians': The Indian Overseas Association

Returning to London in 1917, Polak maintained his relationships, friendships and collegial connections with Indians by correspondence and by occasional visits. His working relationships stretched around the empire. He set up his legal practice in central London chiefly taking cases to the Privy Council for Indians and Indian bodies both in India and across the diaspora. His reputation spread and in 1938, the young Trinidad based lawyer, Mitra Sinanan asked him to take the appeal of Afro-Caribbean labour leader, Uriah Butler against his conviction for sedition. Polak took no fees, working on this successful appeal with Sir Stafford Cripps, the Labour politician and barrister. Both he and Cripps were active in the Labour Party, serving on the party's colonial matters committee, and Polak was a foundation member of the Colonial Advisory Committee of the British Trades Union Congress.[101]

Polak offered his services free of charge in the Privy Council appeal of the young revolutionary socialist Bhagat Singh (1907–1931) condemned to death for the political assassination of a Bengal policeman.[102] He took many cases related to the impact of discriminatory legislation, including the appeal of Queensland cane cutter, Addar Khan, for his conviction under the Queensland Sugar Cultivation Act (1913).[103] Polak acted as the London agent for various Indian organisations such as the National Liberal Federation, the Lucknow Liberal League and nationalist organisations in the feudal princely states, such as the Kathiawar Hitvardhak.[104]

From 1920, alongside his legal work, he set up the London-based Indian Overseas Association (IOA), which took up the cases and causes of Indians across the diaspora, from the Caribbean to East Africa, Australia and Fiji. As secretary Polak was crucial in its foundation and in the prosecution of its aims.[105] He needed a network of information about local conditions in various localities as well as a detailed understanding of local legislation and regulation. He also needed to develop relationships with British officials in the Colonial and India offices. A notion of the global sweep of the issues addressed can be found in his March 1920 report on the first months of the IOA.[106] These included corresponding with the Colonial and India Offices about the Commission concerning the 1919 Asiatics and Trading and Land Act of Transvaal, urging the franchise for qualified Indians in British East Africa, equality of status for Indians and the ending of restrictions on Indian immigration there. He conveyed to the Colonial Office the objection of the East Indian Association of British Guiana to a colonisation scheme as well as pressing for the end of the existing indentures of Indians in Fiji and making representations about indenture to the former German colony of Samoa. Other areas of activity were Ceylon, Mauritius, Australia and Kenya. A Kenyan Indian delegation described him as a 'lidless watcher of India's weal in Britain as well as overseas'.[107]

Polak also connected with young Indian students in Britain and, in 1920, assisted K.T. Paul, the Indian Christian Leader, in founding the YMCA hostel for Indian students in London. Racial prejudice meant Indian students were often refused lodgings and could be under surveillance by British security services. 'Paul wanted this institution to be a space where Indians and British people could meet under conditions of equality'.[108] Polak served on its inter-faith management committee for decades.[109] Along with the East West Friendship Council, he and his family offered hospitality to many Indian students in London. He took young Indian lawyers under his wing, thus arranging Privy Council experience for Barry Sen, later an eminent lawyer and adviser on international affairs.[110]

This activism extended to many organisations during the inter-war years, such as the Quaker sponsored, Indian Conciliation Group, which fostered 'sympathy for the nationalist cause in the British public'.[111] Both the League of Coloured Peoples and the British National Council for Civil Liberties combatted racial discrimination. Despite despairing over the disinterest of the British public in imperial affairs, he gave a series of public lectures in 1923 on issues including the League of Nations, Nationalism and Internationalism, Racial and Colour Problems, and the Necessity of the Brotherhood of Nations, part of his continuing endeavours to educate public opinion towards a more cosmopolitan outlook.[112]

Limits to Cosmopolitanism?

Polak and Gandhi have been criticised by a number of scholars who note their focus upon Indians and neglect of the rights of Africans.[113] Polak referred to the hardship of Indian detainees in the Transvaal having to share prison cells with Africans, 'human beings scarcely emerged from savagery and barbarism, full of animal lusts and brutal passions'.[114] Such opinions echo hierarchical and evolutionary views of humanity, rather than a cosmopolitan and egalitarian one, suggesting a selective anti-racism. However, over time, both Polak and Gandhi widened their views. Indeed, Polak claims that he suggested Gandhi widen his campaign to include the Africans, who were suffering loss of land, violence and discrimination at the hands of the white settler authorities.

> After careful consideration he [Gandhi] decided that it was not advisable to do so, as speaking generally, the Africans were very backward at the time and highly emotional, and would probably not appreciate the necessity of non-violence in thought and action. Besides, he pointed out, whatever the 'passive resisters' gained by their efforts towards racial freedom would be a gain for the Africans, too.[115]

Certainly, there was a tendency within Theosophy to privilege Indians and their religions. Holton notes Annie Besant

> discerned a hierarchy in which the Indians along with the British stood for a higher set of social capacities than the 'savage people and barbarian nations' of most of Africa.[116]

Africans in South Africa pursued their sometimes parallel political goals under the leadership of men such as John Langalibalele Dube (1871–1946) and John Tengo Jabavu (1859–1921), keeping a mutually respectful distance from Gandhi and Polak. But they were located differently under colonialism, with the Indians seeking the end of discriminatory legislation and to enjoy the rights of British subjects and the Africans seeking to hold onto their own land and sovereignty.[117] If Polak focussed early upon the Indian struggles, he later became supportive of African and other peoples. The IOA under Polak's direction, 'was concerned with African as well as Indian welfare. Between the two world wars…the Indian Overseas Association rivalled the Anti-Slavery Society in humanitarian interest in Africa'.[118] Polak with C.F. Andrews and Gandhi were 'instrumental in convincing Indians at home and abroad that Africa belonged to the Africans'.[119]

The recent dismissal of Polak as a 'white do-gooder'[120] fails to consider the complexities of his relationship with Gandhi and their Indian colleagues. Defending Polak from the charge of a British Indian newspaper that he was merely the paid agent of the BIA, Gandhi wrote:

> I know him personally as a dear friend and brother. He came to the cause, embraced poverty and left the Assistant Editorship of a Johannesburg weekly, which might ultimately have proved much to him, if he had desired the goods of this world… The struggle in the Transvaal has meant for Mr. Polak, as it has meant for many Indians, the deprivation of even the means or rather the opportunity of earning a livelihood.[121]

South African Indians appreciated Polak's efforts and dedication. Their farewell, complete with extensive speeches by community leaders, was one of many indications of their regard. A Polak Farewell Committee issued invitations and a flyer, in both English and Gujarati, for his farewell where a special address was presented to him.[122]

Indian liberals valued Polak's connections with them. In 1916, Natesan welcomed him to India saying 'you have sacrificed and laboured for it more than any one of us and you are more Indian in feeling and action than many of us'.[123] In 1917 as Polak prepared to settle back into English life, Surendranath Banerjee, the editor of *The Bengalee*, wrote:

> We won't grudge your settling down to business and living amidst family. We welcome it. You have done enough for us and the country shall never forget your services.[124]

S. Durai Raja Singam, a Malayan Indian, wrote:

> Mr. Polak will always be remembered for his work for Indians overseas, the abolition of Indentured Labour, the betterment of Indo-British relations, the removal of the Race and Colour Bar and the cause of World Unity. His name is a household word among Indians in India, Ceylon and South Africa.[125]

Conclusion

Robert Gregory has written of the costs of Polak's dedication to Indian peoples:

> To champion the welfare of a foreign people against the interests of one's own people, among whom he must continue to live, requires a high degree of imagination, sympathy, dedication, and sacrifice.[126]

Polak was a man who did not understand 'insularity' and felt 'as much "at home", so to speak, "abroad", as I was in the land of my birth'.[127] For Polak, Indian peoples and, indeed, humanity in general were his concern; he saw them equally as sparks 'from an emanation of the Universal self'. His fellow feelings were not confined to the British, but extended globally.

Notes

1. Little has been published on Polak, but see Robert G. Gregory, 'H.S.L. Polak and the Indian Overseas Association', *Vivekananda Kendra Patrika* (Madras) February 1973, pp.33–38, Thomas Weber, *Gandhi as Disciple and Mentor* (Cambridge: Cambridge University Press, 2004), pp. 54–68, Isobel Hofmeyr, *Gandhi's Printing Press* (Cambridge, MA.: Harvard University Press, 2013).
2. Leela Gandhi, *Affective Communities: Anticolonial Thought, Fin-de-Siècle Radicalism, and the Politics of Friendship* (Durham and London: Duke University Press, 2006), p. 7.
3. Marilyn Lake and Henry Reynolds, *Drawing the Global Colour Line* (Melbourne: Melbourne University Press, 2008).
4. Gandhi, *Affective Communities*, p. 3.
5. Paul Gilroy, *Postcolonial Melancholia* (New York: Columbia University Press, 2005), p. 67.

6. Henry Solomon Leon Polak papers (Polak papers), Asian and African collection, British Library. Mss Eur D1238/3.
7. Ibid.
8. Ibid.
9. JonathanSchneer, *London 1900 The Imperial Metropolis* (Yale and London: Yale University Press, 2001), p. 162.
10. Polak papers, Mss Eur D1238/3.
11. Gregory, 'H.S.L. Polak', p. 34.
12. 'Polak Death', *Jewish Chronicle*, 6 February 1959, p. 12.
13. Polak papers, Mss Eur D1238/3.
14. Ibid.
15. Ibid.
16. Ibid.
17. Henry S.L. Polak, 'Indian National Congress', *Indian Review,* January, 1912, p. 94.
18. Ken Weller, *Don't Be a Soldier: The Radical Anti-war Movement in North London, 1914–1918* (London: Journeyman Press, 1985) pp. 85–86.
19. Polak papers, Mss Eur D1238/3.
20. Ibid.
21. Ibid.
22. Ibid, Mss Eur D1238/6.
23. Ibid, Mss Eur D1238/3.
24. R. J. Holton, 'Cosmopolitanism or Cosmopolitanisms: The Universal Races Congress of 1911' *Global Networks,*2, 2(2002), p. 165.
25. The papers of Henry Salomon Leon Polak (PP), MSS. Brit. Emp. s. 372/2, Bodleian Libraries Special Collections, University of Oxford.
26. H.S.L. Polak to M.K. Gandhi, 23 November 1939 at http://gandhiking.ning.com/profiles/blogs/letter-from-h-s-l-polak-november-23-1939-1, accessed 3 December 2013.
27. H.S.L. Polak, 'Brotherhood and War', in S. Durai Raja Singam, (eds) *H.S.L. Polak – Friend of Gandhiji* (Singapore: self-published, 1957), p. 54.
28. H.S.L. Polak, 'Racial Brotherhood' *Hitavada* (Nagpur) 1951 in Singam, p. 70.
29. Polak Papers, Mss.D Eur 1238/1,See *World Conference for International Peace through Religion,* (1937) at http://www.peacepalacelibrary.nl/pmfiles/P04-1-39-040.pdf.
30. Singam, *H.S.L. Polak*, pp. 74–75.
31. Polak papers, Mss Eur D1238/6.
32. Ibid, Mss Eur D1238/3.
33. Hugh Tinker, *A New System of Slavery: The Export of Indian Labour Overseas, 1830–1920,* (Oxford: Oxford University Press, 1974).
34. Lake and Reynolds, *Drawing the Global Colour Line,* pp. 210ff.

35. Ibid, passim.
36. Gregory, 'H.S.L. Polak', p. 34.
37. S.L. (sic) Polak, 'The Origins of Gandhiji's Fasts', *India Bulletin* October 1932, in Singam, pp. 43–44.
38. M.K. Gandhi, *An Autobiography or The Story of My Experiments with Truth* (Ahmedabad: Navajivan, 2005 (1927)), p. 275.
39. Ibid, p.273.
40. Quoted in Weber, *Gandhi*, p. 56.
41. Polak papers, Mss Eur D1238/3.
42. Gandhi, *An Autobiography*, p. 283.
43. PP, MSS Brit. Emp. s372/1/223.
44. Gandhi, *An Autobiography*, p. 283.
45. Robert A. Huttenback, *Gandhi in South Africa: British Imperialism and the Indian Question, 1860–1914* (Ithaca, NY: Cornell University Press, 1971).
46. Uma Dhupelia-Mesthrie, *Gandhi's Prisoner? The Life of Gandhi's Son Manilal* (Delhi: Permanent Black, 2004), p. 76.
47. Uma Mesthrie, 'From Advocacy to Mobilization, *Indian Opinion*, 1903–1914' in Switzer Leo, (ed) *South Africa's Alternative Press: Voices of Protest and Resistance, 1880s–1960s* (Cambridge: Cambridge University Press, 1997), p.116.
48. Weber, *Gandhi,* p. 63.
49. Mesthrie, 'From Advocacy', p. 116.
50. Weber, *Gandhi,* p. 59.
51. Kris, Manjapra, 'Introduction' in Sugata Bose and Kris Manjapra, (eds) *Cosmopolitan Thought Zones, South Asia and the Global Circulation of Ideas* (London: Palgrave MacMillan, 2010), p. 3.
52. Millie Graham Polak, 1931 *Mr. Gandhi: The Man,* Compiled by C.F. Andrews accessed at http://www.mkgandhi.org/ebks/gandhitheman.pdf 21 July 2016, p. 117.
53. Polak papers, Mss Eur D1238/6.
54. Mesthrie, 'From Advocacy', p.112.
55. Hofmyer, *Gandhi's Printing Press*, pp.5, 20.
56. Ibid, p. 72.
57. Ibid.
58. Ibid, p.74.
59. Polak, H.S.L., 'Memories of Gandhi', *Contemporary Review*, 173, January 1948, p. 135.
60. Hofmyer, *Gandhi's Printing Press*, p.117.
61. Anil Nauriya, 'Freedom, Race and Francophonie: Gandhi and the Construction of Peoplehood', *Identity, Culture and Politics*10, 2, 2009, p. 80.
62. PP, MSS. Brit. Emp. s.372/1/60-76.

63. (Madras: Natesan, 1909).
64. Ibid.
65. *Collected Works Mahatma Gandhi,* (CWMG) 98 volumes at http://www.gandhiserve.org/e/cwmg/cwmg.htm accessed 11 September 2016, vol.11, p. 120.
66. 'First Universal Races Congress', *International Journal of Ethics,* 21, 2 January 1911, p. 248.
67. Holton, 'Cosmopolitanism', pp. 153–170.
68. Lake and Reynolds, *Drawing the Global Colour Line,* p. 254.
69. PP, MSS. Brit. Emp. s.372/1/119 121.
70. Polak papers, Mss Eur 1238/1.
71. PP, MSS. Brit. Emp. s.372/2/4-6, Weber, *Gandhi,* p. 66.
72. Polak quoted in Thomas Weber, *Going Native Gandhi's Relationship with Western Women* (New Delhi: Roli Books, 2011), p. 162.
73. Dhupelia-Mesthrie, *Gandhi's Prisoner?,* p. 129.
74. PP, MSS. Brit. Emp. s.372/2/58-61.
75. Henry S.L. Polak, 'Wasted Opportunities in India' *Contemporary Review* 1934, January, p. 542.
76. Ibid, pp. 540–541.
77. Polak quoted in Singam, *H.S.L. Polak,* p.1.
78. Polak Papers, Mss D Eur 1238/1/5.
79. H.S.L. Polak, 'The South African Situation' *Indian Review* (Madras) May 1919, pp. 305–308.
80. Mesthrie, *From Advocacy,* p. 121, Nauriya, 'Freedom, Race', p. 79.
81. Weber, *Gandhi,* p. 54.
82. H. S. L. Polak, 'G. A. N. – Some Happy Memories', *Indian Review,* LI, 1, 1950 p.37.
83. *CWMG,* vol. 9, p. 134.
84. Polak, 'G. A. N.', p.37.
85. Ibid, p.38.
86. Ibid.
87. *CWMG,* vol.8, p. 211.
88. Ibid, vol. 11, p.244.
89. Ibid, vol. 9, p. 405 and vol. 36, pp. 129–130.
90. Ibid, vol. 17, p. 183.
91. Weber, *Gandhi,* p. 61.
92. Gandhi, *An Autobiography,* p. 320.
93. Polak to Gandhi, 23 November 1939.
94. PP, MSS. Brit. Emp. s.372/3/36.
95. *CWMG,* vol. 48, p. 286.
96. Polak to Gandhi, 23 November 1939.
97. *CWMG,* vol. 85, p.55.

98. M.K. Gandhi, *Speeches and Writings of M.K. Gandhi* with an introduction by C.F. Andrews; a tribute by G.A. Natesan; a biographical sketch by H.S.L. Polak (Madras: Natesan, 1910).
99. Singam, *H.S.L. Polak*, p. 2.
100. Polak papers, Mss Eur D1238/6.
101. Sahadeo Basdeo and Brinsley Samaroo, 'Indo-Caribbean Political Leaders during the Twentieth Century' in Parvati Raghuram, Ajaya Kumar Sahoo, Brij Maharaj and Dave Sangha, (eds) *Tracing an Indian Diaspora: Contexts, Memories, Representations* (New Delhi: Sage, 2008), pp. 113–14.
102. Anil Nauriya, 'The Clemency Effort for Bhagat Singh, Sukhdev and Rajguru A Comment', 2012 at https://www.academia.edu/4888156/The_Clemency_Effort_for_Bhagat_Singh_Sukhdev_and_Rajguru accessed 17 July 2016, n.iii.
103. 'Privy Council Appeals', *Sydney Morning Herald*, 6 December 1919, p.13.
104. Gregory, 'H.S.L. Polak', p. 38.
105. Ibid.
106. Henry S.L. Polak, 'Indians (sic) Overseas Association', *Indian Review*, March 1920, p. 212.
107. Quoted in Robert G. Gregory, *India and East Africa A History of Race Relations Within the British Empire1890–1939* (Oxford: Clarendon Press, 1971), p. 238.
108. Nandini Chatterjee, 'The Political Theology of Indian Christian Citizenship: An Instance of Secularism as Culture', in B. Black, G. Hyman, and G. Smith, (eds) *Confronting Secularism in Europe and India: Legitimacy and Disenchantment in Contemporary Times* (London: Bloomsbury, 2014), p. 90.
109. Polak papers, Mss Eur D1238/6.
110. See Raju Ramachandran 'Barry Sen, Counsel's Counsel', *The Wire*, 9 November 2015, at http://thewire.in/15255/barry-sen-counsels-counsel/accessed 15 July 2016.
111. Geoffrey Carnall, *Gandhi's Interpreter: A Life of Horace Alexander* (Edinburgh, 2010), p. 102.
112. PP, MSS. Brit. Emp. s.372/2/3.
113. Ashwin Desai and Goolam Vahed, *Gandhi The South African Stretcher Bearer of Empire* (Stanford: Stanford University Press, 2015).
114. Quoted in Ibid, p. 82.
115. PP, MSS. Brit. Emp. s.372/1/226.
116. Holton, 'Cosmopolitanism', p. 165.
117. Hofmyer, *Gandhi's Printing Press*, Anil Nauriya, *The African Element in Gandhi* (Delhi: National Gandhi Museum and Gyan Publishing House, 2006) at http://www.mkgandhi.org/ebks/The-African-Element-in-Gandhi.pdf accessed 28 July 2016, n.p.

118. Gregory, *India and East Africa*, p. 175.
119. Ibid, p. 237.
120. Desai and Vahed, *Gandhi*, p.83.
121. *CWMG*, vol. 10, p.121.
122. PP, MSS. Brit. Emp. s. 372/2/61ff.
123. Ibid. s.372/2/52.
124. Ibid. s.372/2/59-60.
125. Singam, *H.S.L. Polak* p. 1.
126. Gregory, 'H.S.L. Polak', p. 33.
127. Polak papers, Mss Eur D1238/3.

CHAPTER 4

Provincialised Cosmopolitanisms: Jehangir P. Patel and Marjorie Sykes

Abstract Sometime in the 1980s, two elderly people embarked on a collaboration; a collaboration that affirmed half a lifetime of political fellowship and personal friendship. The result was an English-language book *Gandhi. His Gift of the Fight*. The lives of Marjorie Sykes and Jehangir P. Patel gain historical timbre in the interstices of the larger tale they seek to tell. Two lives take shape in ways that unravel the binaries informing taken-for-granted assumptions about the colonial. They offer a case study of cosmopolitanisms that provincialises the European concept. These provincial cosmopolitanisms did not need to reject a sense of patriotism as a pernicious parochialism. Instead, they inscribed patriotism and nationalism into universalisms that challenged the assumed universalism of European imperialism.

Keywords Provincialised cosmopolitans · Marjorie Sykes · Jehangir P Patel · India · Decolonise · Anti-colonialism

Sometime in the 1980s, two elderly people embarked on a collaboration; a collaboration that affirmed half a lifetime of political fellowship and personal friendship. The result was an English-language book *Gandhi. His Gift of the Fight*[1] published in the tiny Friends Rural Centre in Rasulia, North India. Both authors were well into their eighties at the time. This was an 'end of life' testimony; an offering to the future and perhaps a

J. Haggis et al., *Cosmopolitan Lives on the Cusp of Empire*,
DOI 10.1007/978-3-319-52748-2_4

justification for the values that informed their partnership. The two authors were Marjorie Sykes (1905–1995) and Jehangir P. Patel (1905–n.d.). The book's title suggests a straightforward account of Mahatma Gandhi's struggle for Indian independence. However, entwined within this narrative are the surprising and unexpected stories of the two more obscure figures: the co-authors. Much the same as Sophia Dobson Collet's historical significance emerges in the interplay of her biography of the more famous Ram Mohan Roy and a brief biographical prefix, so the lives of Marjorie Sykes and Jehangir P. Patel gain historical timbre in the interstices of the larger tale they seek to tell. Interspersed between the discussions of big ideas and tumultuous events, two lives take shape in ways that unravel the binaries informing taken-for-granted assumptions about the colonial world[2] and especially anti-colonialism.[3] How had these two people come together? What story lay behind that collaboration? Was this book the product of a 'cosmopolitan thought zone' defined by Manjapra as 'treacherous and provisional shared worlds that arise when disparate groups seek to solve problems together in order to address their pressing concerns.'[4] Building on the critique of cosmopolitanism outlined in Chapter 1, and its application to the transnational networks thrown up on the edges of empire, I suggest that the self-representations of both Sykes and Patel confirm and confront this critique, offering a case study of cosmopolitanisms that provincialise the European concept. These provincial cosmopolitanisms did not need to reject a sense of patriotism as a pernicious parochialism. Instead, they inscribed patriotism and nationalism into universalisms that challenged the assumed universalism of European imperialisms: 'Their cosmopolitanism flowed not from the stratosphere of abstract reason, but from the fertile ground of local knowledge and learning in the vernacular.'[5] These other cosmopolitanisms refused to recognise any false binary of the secular and the religious, while they also challenged the spiritual universals embedded in imperial Christianity. It is to these plural cosmopolitanisms that I turn to consider the coming together of Patel and Sykes in their separate but twinned politico-ethical journeying.

Contrapuntal Histories

The book is a humble little volume of around 250 pages in a plain brown paper cover. Twelve chapters are ordered chronologically, bracketed by a brief introduction and an epilogue. On opening the volume, a black-and-white picture of the heads of Rabindranath Tagore (1861–1941), the Indian Nobel Laureate and anti-colonial nationalist, and Mahatma Gandhi, captioned with the text 'To plant the message of love and courage in a wilderness of hatred and terror,'[6] greets the reader. The picture sums up the purpose of the book better than the title, reinforced by an epigram from Stefan Zweig[7] referring to Romain Rolland[8]: 'One great man who remains human can for ever and for all men rescue our faith in humanity.'[9] This book did not seek to glorify a great man but to use his 'gift' to inspire activism in a contemporary moment the authors describe as 'the tragic eighties' where many young people 'see no future ahead'.[10] This political purpose is reinforced by Hallam Tennyson's preface, a British pacifist and socialist himself,[11] Tennyson affirms the freshness of the book's perspective on 'the well documented' Gandhi by pointing to how 'Marjorie and Jehangir make him real to us once again... once more for the fight'.[12]

The authors' note states the book is 'essentially a record of Gandhi's impact on our own lives' rather than a history or a life story of Gandhi as such.[13] Each of the 12 main chapters interleave political events, the ideas and activisms of the two great men, and how they came to impact on Sykes and Patel individually. Some chapters dwell more on Gandhi and Tagore, their ideas, engagements with each other, and activities, whereas others focus more on the milieus Sykes and Patel inhabited and encountered their ideas. The result is neither biographical nor autobiographical but more of a conversation between and with Gandhi and Tagore's ideas, set against the backdrop of the political struggle against the British. Gandhi was the more visceral, passionate activist, whose spiritual eclecticism was bent to his vision of the Indian masses melded into a self-reliant, non-materialist 'perfect democracy' eschewing private property and the constrictions of caste. He saw this "freeing" of India and Indians as an essential pre-requisite for India's internationalism. Tagore was no less a patriot, but became less and less enamoured of Gandhi's non-violent politics of protest such as satyagraha, and more convinced such tactics fed the particularisms of nationalism and communalism, thus militating against a true universalism.[14] Tagore's absence from the title reflects his influence on only one of the co-authors, Sykes, who 'found that the stimulus of Gandhi... was inextricably intertwined for her with that of Rabindranath Tagore'.[15]

Interestingly, Patel and Sykes structure their own back-stories around the same chronological points as each other, integrating a life cycle trajectory from childhood to maturity into significant moments in India's journey from colonialism to post-colonial independence. Extracted and placed side by side, they constitute a fascinating contrast explored in detail below. However, beyond the book, there is little available evidence with which to contextualise the nature of their collaboration in writing the book. Was it a mutual idea to write the book? How did they arrive at (to the reader) a seamless singular voice, despite the acknowledgement that the book was 'a joint undertaking on the part of two very dissimilar people whose differences of background and temperament have served to enrich their friendship'?[16] How did they determine its structure and form? Or decide how and what to include?

Another set of questions are raised for the historian. What is the status of this text as 'evidence'? Written late in life about two protagonists long since dead, we push historical method to its limits by treating this exercise in self representation and memory as source for an end of empire anti-colonial moment of cosmopolitanism that predates the writing of the book by four or five decades. Where does the fact end and the fiction begin? How much of the book is a desire to make a compelling story for the book's intended contemporary audience, offsetting the 'despair' of the 1980s by offering Gandhi's 'gift' of hope?[17] The very title of the book – an admiring quote from Tagore about Gandhi's rambunctious activism[18] hints at the aspiration of the authors to provide a clarion call to travel 'Gandhi's road... now the only road into a viable future, for India and humanity alike'.[19]

Few sources have thus far surfaced to provide substantive confirmation or refutation of the book's narratives – as history of ideas or as autobiography, especially for Patel. There appears to have been little research focusing on him or personal records in archival repositories. Apart from the details provided in the book, we have to date been able to track down few other sources, beyond a passing reference to him as a leading Parsi who served on the central board of the Reserve Bank of India[20] and extracts from letters written to Patel by Gandhi in the period 1945–1947 compiled by Professor Yogendra Yadav, Gandhi Research Foundation. Yadav acknowledges Patel as 'a famous associate' of the Mahatma who was involved in setting up the All India National Institute of Naturopathy in Pune as part of Gandhi's health program, as confirmed in the book. The letters are largely advising Patel on people he is working with and urging him to persevere at learning Gujarati, with a passing reference to soil improvement.[21] Marjorie Sykes was a published author[22] and a slim biography, drawing heavily on Sykes' own input in letters and conversation, by her friend and fellow Quaker, Martha Dart, was published in 1993.[23] Indeed, in the preface, Dart acknowledges that Sykes largely wrote the chapter on her childhood. The biography confirms many of the details of Sykes' life, but adds little in the way of reflection or insight into Sykes' emotional or spiritual journeys nor is there any mention of her friendship with Patel or the writing of The Gift. Dart subsequently published a book of letters from Sykes to Dart covering the period 1967–1994[24] when Sykes was in retirement but living an active speaking and writing life primarily at Kotagiri, in the Nilgiri Hills of the Western Ghats. These letters are shaped by the nature of the friendship between Dart and Sykes, focussing mainly on keeping in touch with Quaker friends in the UK and USA, soliciting help from Dart in research for the books Sykes wrote during this period; and plotting the movements of Sykes and a seemingly endless stream of visitors to her Indian residence. Frustratingly, only a brief mention is made of Patel and The Gift, in a letter from 21 March 1982, where she sketches who Patel is and that 'The Towls told you about the "Gandhi" book,' closing with the observation that 'Gandhi sent him... on a number of Hindu-Muslim concerns, as he belonged to neither community and had good friends in both'.[25] A deeper insight into their friendship may have to wait until Sykes' personal papers are released by the Library of the Society of Friends in London, currently set at 50 years after death.[26]

Of course, traces, remnants and fragments are part and parcel of the social and cultural historian's modus vivendi. As Steedman eloquently points out 'she is not looking for anything: only silence, the space shaped by what once was; and now is no more'.[27] Memory is perhaps more contentious and challenging if one is reading back to capture an historical moment. However, we aspire less to evoke historical fact than to 'use the analytic advantage of historical hindsight scrupulously to disclose the failure of imperial binarism'[28] through a contrapuntal method. This is defined by Edward Said as 'intertwined and overlapping histories' of colonial contact zones.[29] I unpack Patel and Sykes' singular voice to sit their two autobiographies side by side, not to test or contextualise their veracity but to read them as texts that reveal the myriad confluences through which the binary coloniser/colonised is rendered in polyphonic tones. As Said puts it 'to think through and interpret together experiences that are discrepant... all of them co-existing and interacting with others'.[30]

Lives and Meeting Points

Sykes was the daughter of a schoolmaster from the Yorkshire mining villages who arrived in India via Cambridge University in 1928 to teach at the London Missionary Society's Bentinck Girls High School in Madras. Patel was a son of a wealthy Parsee cotton trading family from Bombay, and also a Cambridge University graduate. They met at Sevagram, Gandhi's rural ashram in Maharashtra, in late 1944, brought together 'by our special interest in the two interlocking programmes which Gandhi was then putting forward as pathways to freedom'.[31] The book sheds little light on how this friendship consolidated itself over the intervening years beyond the testimony of co-authorship. What the book does give is a sense of the life paths that brought them to Sevagram as lieutenants of Gandhi's vision to build Swaraj in the Indian countryside: Sykes through Nai Talim (New Education) and Patel through 'Nature Cure', Gandhi's strategy to bring sustainable health and hygiene to the poor. This fascinating personal and historical trajectory places them within a religio-cultural space trying to articulate new universalisms of the business of living that would serve both a post-colonial India and a post-imperial world.

War and Childhood

Syke's self-representation of her life in the book begins with her everyday life as the eldest child of a Yorkshire schoolmaster, devoted to delivering a good education to the children in the desperately poor mining villages of the West Riding. The year 1914, when she was 9 years old, stands out in her memory as a turning point in her awareness for several reasons.

> War held no glory for me. A beloved teacher disappeared from our school; she was German and had become an 'enemy alien' overnight. We heard talk of the cruel harassment she had suffered from the 'patriotic' hooligans of the town. We children were bewildered, our parents were grieved and angry.[32]
>
> Her father had close friends in Germany from the year he had spent studying in Dresden. Photographs of them hung in the living room of their home and he would often speak of them with affection and wonder how they were and how the war affected them.[33]

These memories reveal an early cosmopolitan influence in her home, where both parents disdain the violent jingoism of the early war years and feel no need to hide their dislike of nationalism and war from their children. Compassion, empathy and sadness mark her familial memories of World War One. Her father returned from the war sad and frustrated with the Versailles Treaty that he correctly predicted would lead to another war. Her mother, exhausted by the strain of it all, became unwell and Sykes spent much of her 14th year at home:

> For the next five months I took charge of the household, cooked and scrubbed, washed the family's clothes, and mended them, got the younger ones off to school, nursed Mother, and in the odd moments tackled the neglected garden a wonderful experience of 'learning through work'.[34]

She would later tell her Indian students that her training in Gandhi's principle of 'learning through living' occurred 'In my own home, by my father and mother'.[35]

In marked contrast to the gritty realism and anti-war sentiment of Sykes' recollections, Patel, also 9 years old in 1914, begins his account of childhood with his memory of watching the Rajput cavalry embarking for France from the Bombay naval docks near his home in Colaba. It was a thrilling scene, as the turbaned soldiers shouted 'British Sarkar Ki Jai' (Victory to the British Raj). He related their cry to the Latin he learned at school 'it is sweet and becoming to die for one's country' (Dulce et decorum Est pro patria mori). For him, as for the Rajputs, Raj and country were the same. His family's lifestyle was very European and English was the language of choice. 'They exemplified, in fact, Macaulay's ideal of an educated Indian as, to all intents and purposes, the "brown Englishman"'.[36] His education at St. Xavier's School, a Jesuit English medium school established in 1869 for sons of the wealthy, regardless of faith, was rigorous but contained little curriculum concerning India. The local languages, Marathi and Gujarati, were considered useful only for conversing with servants and shopkeepers. Cocooned by class and culture, he heard little and knew less of the momentous waves of nationalist fervour sweeping through Bombay and India throughout his childhood.

Cambridge Years 1923–1926

The next stage of their lives which both Sykes and Patel discuss in the book, is their time at university. Despite her interrupted education (she had also survived a bout of Spanish influenza), Sykes entered Newnham College,

Cambridge, in 1923 to major in English. Those 3 years were crucial in shaping her life path spiritually, politically and professionally. It was here, she records in the book, that she first heard about Gandhi from Indian students who had participated in the non-cooperation movement several years earlier.[37] However, of more impact on her at the time was that it was here too she found Christianity and faith (her family were not practicing Christians). It was a version of Christianity shaped by a post-war generation of teachers and thinkers determined to link Christianity to the burning issues of their time: peace and social justice.

> Cambridge led me to see that the way of Jesus was a way of 'non-violence' – a way to be followed in the details of daily living. Jesus, not Gandhiji, was my teacher of truth and non-violence; although what I learned in Cambridge was confirmed and much enriched by what I learned later from Gandhiji and others in India.[38]

Through the Student Christian Movement (SCM),[39] she also encountered international Christian students from Europe, North America and elsewhere who were critiquing the negative attitudes to local cultures held by Christian missionaries (some of whom were their own parents). She 'became aware that the message of Jesus must be given with respect for the various cultural traditions of the world and a readiness to learn from them'.[40] Her decision to complete a postgraduate teaching diploma was informed by the young teachers from universities and schools around the world who visited Cambridge under the auspices of the SCM to invite Cambridge men and women to be equal partners with them in the education of their own people. This was not an invitation to colonise the mind, but to help ensure 'their cultures were to be enriched and not destroyed by their contact with the west'.[41] She quotes a phrase of Dr. Aggrey, founder of Achimota College, Accra, Ghana: 'the piano needs both its black keys and its white ones to evoke the full music'.[42] It was in this spirit that Sykes accepted the teaching position with the London Missionary Society at the Bentinck School in Madras.

In 1921 the 16-year-old Patel was sent to England to live with an Indian friend of the family in Cambridge while attending 2 years of preparatory school to ready himself for university entrance exams. He arrived at Downing College to read natural sciences at the same time Sykes entered Newnham College to read English, although their paths did not cross. For him, Cambridge was less a place of spiritual awakening or international awareness than a place of society and (mainly) acceptance. He felt quite at home in Downing. He liked the English students, while the numerous Indian students congregated mainly around sport, especially cricket and tennis. It was here he felt the first stirrings of national pride as an Indian, when 'A great cricketer and an even greater gentleman', Duleep Singh[43] was refused membership to a university sporting club. Patel reacted angrily and, with his Indian associates, organised a counter-club and imposed a reverse colour bar.[44] This was, however, the exception that proved the rule: to him England remained a second home and he describes himself as '...still in many ways a typical "brown Englishman"' on his return to Bombay and the family business in 1926.[45]

India 1928–1937 Apprenticeship

Arriving in Madras at the height of public protests against the Simon Commission and its lack of Indian representation,[46] Sykes could hardly avoid the anti-colonial struggle, even if she had been so minded. Through existing networks in the Madras Christian community, Marjorie was soon introduced to the International Fellowship in Chennai, an organisation inspired by Gandhi's insistence on not treating the British as enemies: 'Part we must, but as friends'.[47] This was the core of his non-violence theory of anti-colonial struggle. The Fellowship

> ...tried to follow this principle and to demonstrate in practice that Indian and English people could be good friends, and learn to understand each other's point of view, even though they might come to different conclusions. Many said this was impossible, but in fact Indians of a great variety of religious and political outlook were attracted into the fellowship, as well as British and other foreign residents.[48]

It was at a Fellowship meeting that Sykes met C. Rajagopalachariar[49] (Rajaji), Gandhi's chief worker in Tamil Nadu. Through Rajaji, she learned about Gandhi's practical program to build a 'new India'; learned to spin; and heard first-hand of the struggle against untouchability.

The Bentinck School was not unaffected by the anti-colonial movement. Other staff members shared her growing interest in the ideas of Gandhi and Tagore. The school adopted practices designed to prepare their students for Swaraj, 'responsible freedom', by instituting a cooperative rather than competitive environment and actively resisting caste and other distinctions:

> The children themselves swept and cleaned the buildings and compound, and cared for class gardens and libraries, learning the responsibilities of citizenship.[50]

Sykes also took seriously the problem of language, instituting a policy of 'Tamil first, English second' in the curriculum during her headship, which she assumed in 1930. It was a long-standing issue for Indian nationalists that English was considered the pre-eminent language of instruction, knowledge and civilised culture since at least Macaulay's Minute on Education of 1835 which institutionalised the superiority of English and European culture in India. While female education was much slower to develop and to institutionalise English as the preferred language for instruction, by the late 1920s most elite girls' schools were English medium. Even religious education was touched by Swaraj. Although the School's spiritual core was a Christian one, Sykes

> [E]njoyed teaching about biblical prophets who stood against public corruption and the oppression of the poor was related to India's aspirations for social justice and national integrity.[51]

In contrast to Sykes' recollections of streets full of waving black flags protesting against the Raj, Patel's return to Bombay is couched in terms of loneliness and alienation. Gandhi was a name he heard occasionally, when passing the train station, as passengers on the local trains shouted slogans about boycotting British goods and victory for Gandhi. It was only when he discovered other Cambridge and Oxford educated men, many of whom were lawyers, that he felt more at home. Joining the Bar Gymkhana[52] brought him directly into the sphere of Bombay's nationalist leaders, including Jinnah, the leader of the All-India Muslim League and the eventual founder of Pakistan; and the debates that were raging over what form a newly independent Indian nation should take. He became a close friend and admirer of M. C. Chagla, a Muslim and passionate advocate of a secular democracy who nevertheless agreed with Gandhi that a secular state could be rooted in religiosity.[53] It was under Chagla's guidance that 'Jahangir began to think as an Indian, and no longer to look at India from a British point of view', suggestive also of how he no longer saw himself perhaps in terms solely of his membership of the Parsi community.[54]

The turning point for Patel in his commitment to the anti-colonial movement was 1929. Urged by his brother to find out more about the family's cotton business, he embarked on a tour of cotton-growing districts in the various parts of India from which the business sourced its cotton. It was his first real experience of rural India and he was shocked at the level of poverty and the contempt with which the poor were treated, which he experienced first-hand when he tried to rescue a woman road worker suffering through the last stages of tuberculosis. To the astonished incomprehension of the foreman, Patel removed the woman to his car caring for her as well as he could until she died in his arms.

> 'Why worry? If one dies, there are hundreds more waiting to take her place' commented the bemused foreman.
>
> 'What does the British Raj have to say about that?' retorted Patel.
>
> 'The White Sahibs? Oh, they say the same: what does it matter?' came the response.[55]

He 'was expected, being a "monied" man, to share their callous attitude towards the poor' despite the unapologetic racism of local British officials and civilians in the district towns who excluded him from their clubs.[56] Reading Gandhi's autobiography, *The Story of My Experiments with Truth*[57] confirmed his allegiance but he was caught in a dilemma as to how best to serve the cause, especially as the death of his brother meant both family and business responsibilities would increase. He decided to seek out the man himself to ask his advice, to the bemusement of Gandhi's staff when the young prosperous businessman turned up requesting an appointment; one went so far as to warn him that such a meeting might really upset his life.

Jahangir's meeting with Gandhi, recounted in detail in the book, turned on the fact that he could not converse in Gandhi's native tongue of Gujarati. He admitted he spoke it badly and was much more fluent in English. Somewhat defensively he explained that the English were good people and that he owed them a great deal.

> 'I haven't found anyone here yet with whom I can feel so much at home as I do with my English friends. We Parsees aren't good Indians, you know.'
>
> 'Is that true?' asked Gandhi. 'What about Dadabhai Naoroji?.... Pherozeshah Mehta?[58] Weren't they good Indians? What about you?'
>
> 'What do you mean by a good Indian?'... 'Are you a good Indian??' asked Jahangir.[59]

The conversation closed with Gandhi's emphatic declaration that 'India's spine is bent double under this load of poverty. It makes her servile. I want to see her walk upright and free'.[60]

1938–1948 Maturity

As her knowledge of, and interest in, Gandhi's educational ideas grew, and the politics of communalism took stronger root in the Independence movement, Sykes felt the constraints of working within a government educational system and an institution based on overt Christian agency. By this time, through her membership of the International Fellowship, she had also come into contact with Quakers for the first time. Her biographer describes the attraction thus:

> She found that Quakers believed that an essential part of the way of Jesus was that peace, justice and righteousness should be expressed in practical living – ideas that had so attracted her at Cambridge. She responded to the Quaker belief that in all human beings of whatever race or creed, there is something that enables them to recognise and respond to 'the Truth', 'a Light within', 'an inward teacher'.[61]

She formally professed as a Quaker while on furlough in England in 1936.

Through the offices of a Quaker friend, Sykes accepted an invitation from Tagore to work as a lecturer to Santiniketan in December 1938. On her journey to Bengal, she also visited Gandhi's ashram at Segaon, Eastern Maharashtra, and had her first meeting with him and saw his educational ideas in practice. Although she had doubts about the value of quite so much time spent spinning, she was impressed at the liveliness of the children and their knowledgeable discussions of the cotton they grew, carded and spun; proof of 'the educational value of doing ordinary work scientifically'.[62] She was similarly impressed at Santiniketan where she observed the school children combining research and service in the village health centre. The war disrupted her time at Santiniketan, bringing her back to mainstream education to help out at the Madras Women's Christian College. The principal, Eleanor Rivett, was in desperate need of an English teacher as wartime conditions prevented staff being sent from England.[63] It also brought her back into the maelstrom of the Quit India campaign, where the students took up Gandhi's call for non-violent Swaraj by growing their own food sufficient to share with women and children in a Madras slum where Sykes was living, at the rear of a kindergarten she had established. By the end of the war, Sykes was back at Santiniketan, although increasingly caught up in the cross-flow with Segaon and Gandhi's work.

For Patel, these years saw him finally commit to direct engagement in the anti-colonial movement and Gandhi's program of building Swaraj from the bottom up. He was influential in engineering the Bombay Cotton Exchange's support for the freedom movement, despite boycotts directly impacting on their bottom line. He also came into contact with advocates of Gandhi's work among the poor: Verrier Elwin, an Oxford don now devoted to working among the Adivasi (indigenous tribal communities) of Gondwana, and Amritlal V. Thakkar (Thakkar Bapa) who worked among the 'untouchable' sweepers of Bombay. He was also sufficiently active to be shadowed by the police according to him, although to date we have not been able to verify this through archival sources. In 1940, Patel joined the newly established Adivasi Seva Mandel (Aboriginals Service Society) in Thane District under the auspices of Gandhi and Thakkar Bapa. The Mandel worked among the tribal peoples (Warli and Katkari) to develop health and educational services, labourers' cooperatives and housing.

By the time Sykes and Patel met, in late 1944, they were caught up in Gandhi's grand vision for constructing a 'non-violent democracy' that took Swaraj beyond simply 'brown-skin' rule in Delhi[64] This grass-roots democracy, in Gandhi's words,

> … must touch every aspect of daily living and help every man and woman to be a better citizen of their village, and therefore a better citizen of India and the world. It must inculcate a spirit of neighbourliness which would rise above narrower loyalties and do away with untouchability and with communal jealousies and suspicions.[65]

Here we see how Gandhi weaves the local through the national to a cosmopolitan global mindset, melding not only villagers, or Indians, but humanity, into a single community of fellow-feeling.

In 1945, this was the vision that Gandhi attempted to implement in Segaon village. It was to be the 'spear-head of a silent social revolution'[66] based on the twin programs of Nai Talim (Basic Education)[67] and Nature Health.[68] It was to this revolutionary ideal that Sykes and Patel committed themselves. Sykes accepted Gandhi's invitation to join the Nai Talim effort in Segaon, although she did not actually take up the post until after Gandhi's death in 1948. Patel was recruited to the Nature Cure program – intended to develop and make available effective non-Western health remedies along with preventative education in nutrition and hygiene to the poor in keeping with the principles of self-reliance that underpinned Gandhi's notion of Swaraj. In late 1945, Gandhi, Dr. Dinshaw Mehta[69] and Patel established the All India Nature Cure Foundation, whose mission was to deliver 'the benefits of nature cure' nationwide.[70]

Conclusion: Provincialised Cosmopolitanisms?

To what extent do Sykes and Patel reflect examples of provincialised and aspirational cosmopolitanisms? To what extent are they local and vernacular?

Sykes' boundary crossing and her commitment to Swaraj is constructed out of her local knowledge of the transformational struggle against poverty and class performed in her father's ethical practice. It is given a spiritual cast in the Cambridge of the 1920s, scarred by the first world war, as she responds to an intellectual push away from an imperial evangelism to an ecumenical Christianity capable of building a new world in practical partnership with other peoples and faiths. Religion is her way into a shared space in its most universalist sense: the meeting of people committed to humanness as inextricably material and spiritual. She quotes Gandhi to explain her profession of Quakerism at the point at which she moves out of the Christian and into the 'Indian' context:

> Mankind is one and I'm a servant of mankind. I'm born an Indian; I try to be a good Indian in order that I may be a good member of the human race. I'm also born Hindu, and as a loyal Hindu, I claim my passport, so that I may move freely and in friendship among people of every religion.[71]

To Sykes this illustrated how faith and nation could come together in universal comity and cosmopolitan amity. Sykes' spiritual passport takes literal shape, however, in her assumption of Indian citizenship in 1948, tangling the universalist and the particularistic in ways unimagined by European political thought on cosmopolitanism that presumes an inherent particularism in nationalism.[72] She spent the next 20 years intertwining efforts to train teachers in Gandhian Basic Education at Sevagram, with activism in the international peace movement, including a 3-year stint in Nagaland,[73] north-east India, as an observer in a peace keeping effort initiated by Jayaprakash Narayan,[74] a leading Indian political thinker and activist. Interestingly, Narayan convinced Sykes she had a unique role to play there because, on the one hand, the national government knew her as a 'pre-Independence friend' and would give her the necessary permit, while the Naga leaders would 'accept you as a fellow Christian, and not an Indian by birth'.[75] Here Sykes's 'rootless' cosmopolitanism constructs her political utility as the ideal Gandhian observer. Until late old age, she spent the rest of her life living in India, running small peace training camps, researching and writing books on the Quakers in India amongst other topics, and speaking on the importance of Gandhian values for an anti-violence way of life. After ill health increasingly restricted her activities, she finally retired to Swarthmore, a Quaker retirement community in the English Cotswolds, in January 1991.

Patel's story is superficially less cosmopolitan; he has to shuck off the glamour of Englishness and view of England as his second home and 'decolonize' his mind through re-nationalising himself. Encountering rural India's poverty for the first time, at least emotionally, when he holds the dying road worker in his arms, and inspired by his fellow elite friends, Patel gradually immerses himself in the Indian struggle to be an independent nation. Gandhi's exhortations urging him to learn his own vernaculars hint at the struggles this involved for Patel, expressing how displaced he felt in 'Indian India'. In a letter to Patel dated 16 January 1946, Gandhi wrote: 'I have your letter dictated in chaste Gujerati. I am delighted. However, … I shall certainly write in English if that helps us better.'[76] Towards the end of the book, Patel recounts his experience on a trade mission to Japan in 1947 that he undertook at the urging of Gandhi despite his own fears of partition and his desire to remain in India to fight against such a possibility, a fear pooh-poohed by Gandhi. For Gandhi it was an opportunity to present 'the claims of non-violence' to General MacArthur.[77] Whether he had this opportunity is not revealed by Patel; instead, his focus is on his sadness at seeing the Japanese brought so low by their American conquerors and the devastation of Hiroshima. A meeting with two Japanese nuclear scientists, personally horrified 'by the prostitution of scientific discovery to military uses' is couched in terms of a talk with 'fellow-Asians, interested in the welfare of all Asia's people equally'.[78] The brown Englishman is now a pan-Asian through his identification with the particularities of nation and people. It is his sense of Indian-ness, fostered over the years after his return from Cambridge, that brings him to Japan and a sense of a shared identity with 'fellow Asians', rather than a 'brown gentleman's' sense of community with a British elite. This is precisely what Bose suggests is at the core of 'colourful cosmopolitanisms': a 'universalist patriotism' forged in a colonized world that 'refuses to recognize any false binary'.[79]

Notes

1. Jehangir P. Patel and Marjorie Sykes, *Gandhi: His Gift of the Fight* (Rasulia: Friends Rural Center, 1987).
2. Marilyn Lake, 'Chinese Colonists Assert Their 'Common Human Rights': Cosmopolitan as Subject and Method of History,' *Journal of World History* 21, no. 3 (September 2010): 375–92, doi: 10.1353/jwh.2010.0011.
3. Leela Gandhi, *Affective Communities: Anticolonial Thought, Fin-de-Siècle Radicalism, and the Politics of Friendship* (Duke University Press, 2005).
4. Kris Manjapra, 'Introduction', *Cosmopolitan Thought Zones: South Asia and the Global Circulation of Ideas*, eds. Sugata Bose and Kris Manjapra (Basingstoke: Palgrave Macmillan, 2010), 1.
5. Sugata Bose, 'Different Universalisms, Colorful Cosmopolitanisms: The Global Imagination of the Colonized,' in *Cosmopolitan Thought Zones: South Asia and the Global Circulation of Ideas*, ed. Sugata Bose and Kris Manjapra (Basingstoke: Palgrave Macmillan, 2010), 97.
6. Lion M. G. Agarwal, *Freedom Fighters of India*, volume 2 (New Delhi LISHA Books, 2008), 195; Bal Ram Nanda, *Gandhi: A Pictorial Biography* (New Delhi: Publications Division, Ministry of Information and Broadcasting, 1972).
7. Stefan Zweig (1881–1942) was an Austrian Jewish author whose fame was at its height in the 1920s and 1930s. His works were widely translated, although his reputation was never as great amongst English reading publics. He was an internationalist and Europeanist who fled Europe first in 1934 to London, then to the USA in 1939 before finally settling in Brazil where he and his wife committed suicide in despair at the destruction of the European culture they saw as theirs. Leo Carey, 'The Escape Artist: The Death and Life of Stefan Zweig,' *The New Yorker*, August 27, 2012; see also Oliver

Matuschek, *Three Lives: A Biography of Stefan Zweig*, trans. Allan Blunden (London: Pushkin Press, 2013).

8. Romain Rolland (1866–1944) was a French writer, winner of the 1915 Nobel Prize for Literature, he was a pacifist, internationalist and mystic who corresponded with Rabindranath Tagore and published a book on Gandhi; *Mahatma Gandhi: The Man Who Became One with the Universal Being*, trans. Catherine Daae Groth (New York: The Century Co., 1924).
9. Stefan Zweig, *Romain Rolland: The Man and His Work*, trans. Eden Paul and Cedar Paul (New York: Thomas Seltzer, 1921), 356.
10. Patel and Sykes, introduction to *Gandhi: His Gift of the Fight*, 2.
11. Hallam Tennyson (1920–2005) was a 'pacifist-Marxist' writer and BBC radio producer, as well as great grandson of Alfred, Lord Tennyson, the Victorian poet laureate. He and his wife spent 2 years in India in the late 1940s, including several months in Gandhi's ashram, where he met Gandhi and probably Marjorie Sykes who was living at the ashram then. It is unclear whether or when he met Patel. Ann Thwaite, 'Obituary: Hallam Tennyson', *Independent*, January 2, 2006, http://www.independent.co.uk/news/obituaries/hallam-tennyson-521322.html, accessed 24 September 2016.
12. Hallam Tennyson, preface to *Gandhi: His Gift of the Flight*, by Jehangir P. Patel and Marjorie Sykes (Rasulia: Friends Rural Center, 1987), ix.
13. Patel and Sykes, authors' note to *Gandhi: His Gift of the Fight*, xi.
14. Suresh Sharma, 'Swaraj and the Quest for Freedom – Rabindranath Tagore's Critique of Gandhi's Non-Cooperation,' *Thesis Eleven* 39, no. 1 (August 1994): 93–104; T. S. Rukmani, 'Tagore and Gandhi,' in *Indian Critiques of Gandhi*, ed. Harold Coward (Albany: SUNY Press, 2003), 107–128.
15. and Sykes, authors' note to *Gandhi: His Gift of the Fight*, xi.
16. Ibid.
17. Patel and Sykes, introduction to *Gandhi: His Gift of the Fight*, 2.
18. Ibid.
19. Ibid.
20. arZan, 'The Parsis and the Reserve Bank of India Connections,' *Parsi Khabar* (blog), September 30, 2014, http://parsikhabar.net/finance/the-parsis-and-the-reserve-bank-of-india-connections/8556/.
21. Yogendra Yadav, 'Jehangir Patel and Mahatma Gandhi,' *Prof. Dr. Yogendra Yadav's Blog, The Gandhi-King Community*, April 25, 2013, http://gandhiking.ning.com/profiles/blogs/jehangir-patel-and-mahatma-gandhi-1.
22. Sykes has authored a number of written works, primarily books as well as some journal articles. Notable ones include:

    Banarsidas Chaturvedi and Marjorie Sykes, *Charles Freer Andrews: A Narrative.* (London: George Allen & Unwin, 1949).

Sykes, Marjorie, *Rabindranath Tagore* (London: Longmans, Green & Co., 1943).

Sykes, Marjorie, *The Earth Is the Lord's: Shri-Vinoba Bhave and the Land* (London: Friends Peace Committee, 1952).

Sykes, Marjorie, *The Story of Rabindranath Tagore* (Bombay: Orient Longmans, 1950).

23. Martha Dart, *Marjorie Sykes: Quaker Gandhian* (Syracuse, NY: Syracuse University Press, 1993).
24. Majorie Sykes, *In Quaker Friendship: Letters from Marjorie Sykes*, ed. Martha Dart (York: William Sessions Ltd., 1999).
25. Ibid, 78.
26. 'About the collections,' Quakers in Britain, accessed May 30, 2016, http://www.quaker.org.uk/resources/library/about-the-collections. Last paragraph of the subsection 'Archives and manuscripts'.
27. Carolyn Steedman, *Dust* (Manchester: Manchester University Press, 2001), 154.
28. Leela Gandhi, introduction to *Affective Communities: Anticolonial Thought, Fin-de-Siècle Radicalism, and the Politics of Friendship* (Durham: Duke University Press, 2006), 3.
29. Edward Said, *Culture and Imperialism* (London: Chatto & Windus, 1993), 19.
30. Ibid, 36.
31. Patel and Sykes, *Gandhi: His Gift of the Fight*, 135.
32. Dart, *Marjorie Sykes*, 5.
33. Ibid, 6.
34. Ibid, 7.
35. Patel and Sykes, introduction to *Gandhi: His Gift of the Fight*, 5.
36. Ibid, 4.
37. Marjorie was a member of Newnham College at Cambridge, where friends introduced her to what Dart describes as a 'flourishing university society known as "international teas"' often held at a friend's home.

    'Students from all over the world filled the big drawing room; there were many from India, including two or three women from Madras who were to make Marjorie welcome there a few years later. A number of the Indians had been active in Mahatma Gandhi's first "non-cooperation movement" two years earlier, and the name Gandhi became familiar to Marjorie for the first time'. Dart, *Marjorie Sykes*, 13.
38. Dart, *Marjorie Sykes*, 13.
39. The Student Christian Movement was established in the UK in 1889 as a network of students dedicated to missionary work overseas. However, by the turn of the century, it was pioneering Christian internationalisms far more

liberal than imperial evangelicalism. It became the largest student organisation in Britain and was a major influence for ecumenicalism in the early twentieth century and was a prime mover for the Edinburgh World Missionary Conference in 1910 see Tissington Tatlow, *The Story of the Student Christian Movement of Great Britain and Ireland* (London: SCM Press, 1933).

40. Dart, *Marjorie Sykes*, 16.
41. Ibid, 17.
42. Patel and Sykes, introduction to *Gandhi: His Gift of the Fight*, 8.
43. Ibid, 6. The book misspells Duleepsinhji's name. Kumar Shri Duleepsinhji (1905–1959) was from the princely Rajput family of Nawanagar, now part of Gujarat. His uncle, K.S. Ranjitsinhji (1872–1933) was the more famous cricketer but Duleepsinhji played for Cambridge and Sussex in the 1920s and 30s (see his entry in the Wisden Cricket Almanac for 1930, 'Kumar Shri Duleepsinhji,' http://www.espncricinfo.com/wisdenalmanack/content/story/154691.html, accessed September 24, 2016). Duleepsinhji went on to become a High Commissioner to Australia from 1951–1954.
44. Ibid.
45. Ibid.
46. The Simon Commission, officially the Indian Statutory Commission, chaired by Sir John Simon, was sent to India in 1928 by the British Government to investigate the possibility of constitutional reform. Public protest centred on its complete lack of Indian representation – all seven members were British MPs – and it was boycotted by the Indian National Congress. Major public protests greeted it at every city it visited as well as strikes. Visually arresting masses of black flags were waved by the throngs protesting against the Commission's authority.
47. Patel and Sykes, *Gandhi: His Gift of the Fight*, 32.
48. Ibid.
49. At this time, Rajagopalachariar was a leading member of the INC and served as the Chief Minister of Madras as well as becoming the first and last Indian Governor-General and holding ministries in the national government after Independence.
50. and Sykes, *Gandhi: His Gift of the Fight*, 45.
51. Ibid, 48.
52. The Bar Gymkhana appears to be a reference to the Bombay (now Mumbai) Gymkhana, an elite sporting club founded in 1875 and still in operation. Membership was restricted to Europeans until well into the 1930s. Cricket was a major focus of its activities amongst other sports. Parsees were amongst the earliest communities to take up the sport and play against British teams. It is possible Patel is referring to one of the communal Gymkhanas that were established in Bombay; as Majumdar documents,

there were a number of Parsee clubs in Bombay in the early 19th century with cricket as a focus: Boria Majumdar, 'Cricket in Colonial India: The Bombay Pentangular, 1892–1946,' *The International Journal of the History of Sport* 19, no. 2–3 (2002): 157–188. For a recent analysis of the role of the club in colonial society, see Benjamin B. Cohen, *In the Club: Associational Life in Colonial South Asia* (Manchester University Press, 2015).
53. Chagla was secretary of the Muslim League in 1927–28.
54. Patel and Sykes, *Gandhi: His Gift of the Fight*, 35.
55. Ibid, 37.
56. Ibid, 124.
57. Originally published in weekly instalments in Gandhi's journal *Navjivan* from 1925–1929, it also appeared in English in his other journal Young India. The first book edition was published in 1927.
58. Both Bombay Parsees active from the 1870s in the nationalist movement and the early INC.
59. Ibid, 38.
60. Ibid, 40.
61. Dart, *Marjorie Sykes*, 21.
62. Patel and Sykes, *Gandhi: His Gift of the Fight*, 54.
63. Dart, *Marjorie Sykes*, 29.
64. Patel and Sykes, *Gandhi: His Gift of the Fight*, 124.
65. Ibid.
66. Ibid, 132.
67. '... the transformation of human relationships toward healing a wholeness, of human society' Patel and Sykes, *Gandhi: His Gift of the Fight*, 135–136.
68. Ibid, 119.
69. Mehta was an associate of Gandhi who founded and ran the National Institute of Naturopathy in Pune, India.
70. Patel and Sykes, *Gandhi: His Gift of the Fight*, 120–121.
71. Ibid, 39.
72. See particularly the discussion in Bose, 'Different Universalisms, Colorful Cosmopolitanisms', 97–102.
73. Nagaland, a region bordering Myanmar and the state of Assam, consists of a number of different ethnic groups under the umbrella name of Nagas. Distinctive ethnically and historically from the sub-continent, the Nagas sense of separateness from India was nurtured under British rule and reinforced by a wholesale conversion to Christianity and education in English. At Independence, the Nagas declared themselves independent from the new Indian state and began a long-running insurgent struggle for national autonomy. Despite Nagaland being made a state of the Indian union in 1963, and numerous peace initiatives and agreements, the Naga insurgency has continued although currently a fragile peace stems from an accord between the main

insurgent group and the Indian government signed in August 2015. See Alex Waterman, 'Premature Prospects for Peace in Nagaland,' *ISIS Voices* (blog), *International Institute of Strategic Studies*, March 4, 2016, https://www.iiss.org/en/iiss-voices/blogsections/iiss-voices-2016-9143/march-71d7/nagaland-peace-process-89fd; and Dinesh Kotwal, 'The Naga Insurgency: The Past and the Future,' *Strategic Analysis* 24, no. 4 (2008): 751–772.

74. Jayaprakash Narayan (1902–1979) was a leading socialist activist in the anti-colonial nationalist movement in India before Independence. After Independence, he helped found the Praja Socialist Party but retired from politics in 1953 to join the Sarvodaya movement for social reconstruction in the countryside, during which period he became acquainted with Sykes. He returned to politics in the 1970s to lead the opposition to Mrs Indira Gandhi and the Congress Party's anti-democratic Emergency. Brass, Paul, 'Narayan, Jayaprakash'. Paul R. Brass, 'Narayan, Jayaprakash (1902–1979),' in *Oxford Dictionary of National Biography* (Oxford University Press, 2004–), accessed September 25, 2016, doi: 10.1093/ref:odnb/47755.
75. Dart, *Marjorie Sykes*, 51.
76. Mahatma Gandhi to Jehangir P. Patel, Bombay, January 16, 1946, in *The Collected Works of Mahatma Gandhi, 1945–1946* (Ahmedabad: Navajivan Trust, 1980), 431.
77. Patel and Sykes, *Gandhi: His Gift of the Fight*, 156.
78. Ibid, 159.
79. Bose, 'Different Universalisms, Colorful Cosmopolitanisms,' 99.

CHAPTER 5

Cosmopolitan Modernity and Post-imperial Relations: Dominion Australia and Indian Internationalism in the Interwar Pacific

Abstract In the penultimate chapter, this book turns to a range of cosmopolitan internationalisms active in transnational networks of the interwar Pacific. Indian and Australian cosmopolitans who were visitors in each other's countries and delegates at the same international conferences epitomise the mobility and interpersonal exchange that characterises many of the cosmopolitan thought zones discussed in previous chapters. While their international activities in the interwar Pacific, linking interpersonal cosmopolitanisms with the ideal of world government in this era, offer further insight into the range of shared if also divergent grounds upon which cosmopolitanism thought zones formed and through which a variety of interconnected post-imperial worlds continued to be imagined following World War 1.

Keywords Pan-Pacific internationalism · White Australia · Cross-cultural exchange · Theosophy

In its final chapter this book turns to a range of cosmopolitan internationalisms active in transnational networks operating out of the interwar Pacific. Indian and Australian cosmopolitans who were visitors in each other's countries and delegates at the same international conferences epitomise the mobility and interpersonal exchange that characterises many of the cosmopolitan thought zones discussed in the previous

J. Haggis et al., *Cosmopolitan Lives on the Cusp of Empire*,
DOI 10.1007/978-3-319-52748-2_5

chapters. Their international activities in the interwar Pacific offer further insight into the range of shared and divergent grounds upon which cosmopolitanism thought zones formed over our period of investigation and through which a variety of interconnected post-imperial worlds were imagined.

Indeed, the proliferation of non-government movements and networks in the 1920s and 1930s can be seen as a bridge between the affective cosmopolitanisms interwoven through the pages of this book, and the ideal of world government that gained traction following World War 1. Given official internationalism at the League of Nations and the International Labour Organisation was limited to official government representation, myriad non-government experts, commentators, activists and visionaries set about creating their own collaborative spaces. 'India' and Indians were part of this interwar international landscape.[1] The cosmopolitan thought zones created and embodied by such internationalists built upon a Christian liberal progressive project to modernise interracial and intercultural relations through encouraging dialogue between 'East and West'. Thus, the Institute of Pacific Relations (IPR) established in 1925 constitutes a leading example of the many educational and missionary non-government organisations and networks, some already discussed in this book, that set out to facilitate the formation of intersecting cosmopolitan worldviews between individuals and societies considered to be otherwise culturally, racially and historically divided.

The reform of laissez-faire capitalism was one such area for collaborative thinking. As Tomoko Akami has shown in her study of the IPR, in the interwar decades, the conditions of modern capital were a key topic among progressives concerned to debate the future of international relations.[2] By the late 1920s, the rise of fascism and a world crisis in capitalism had complicated hopes that old-style colonial and race relations would be replaced by indirect rule. As the end of empire seemed indefinitely postponed, how to manage economic development in the colonial world exercised both sides of the colonial divide. According to Ritu Birla, by the 1920s, British liberals anticipated the arrival of new Economic Man in India, for example.[3] While most obviously among Indian nationalists, Gandhi's self-rule movement espoused the ideals of rural communitarianism. Communitarianism had been circulating, however, from the 1890s through G.K. Gokhale's organisation, The Servants of India. According to C.A. Bayly, Gokhale promoted rural industrialism in India but also predicted a degree of urban industrialisation that would only become reality under Nehru in the post-independence era.[4]

The importance of 'India' to the 'East-West' agenda of the Pan-Pacific movement has been largely overlooked. Yet India was a key example of the modernising East that the IPR sought to incorporate within its progressive agenda. With Japan and China already independent nations, it was assumed India would soon achieve Dominion status within the British Commonwealth. Moreover, Indian indenture in Fiji and elsewhere in the Pacific was a cause of humanitarian concern that numbered among the 'problems of the Pacific' that Pan-Pacific internationalists sought to solve. They were also concerned with the 'Indian problem' of over-population, poverty, and lack of mass education, which they saw as limiting the capacity for India to modernise. Until that cycle was broken, Western commentators predicted that indenture would continue and independence would remain deferred. The second half of this chapter investigates debates about labour and reform in India and China at the IPR conference in Japan in 1929. As argued below, the process of exchanging views on industrialisation revealed both the limits of cosmopolitanism aspired to by participants, and their shared investment in international dialogue to shape a post-imperial world.

One of the filaments holding these discussions together was the emphasis on faith, which remained intrinsic to liberal social scientific accounts of the future of humankind. As Tamsin Peitch has noted, the social science focus of twentieth-century international networks built upon, rather than superseded, religious networks from the nineteenth century.[5] In this way, Young Men's and Women's Christian Associations in Asia, including in India, inspired the formation of the IPR in the mid-1920s. The Indian and Australian internationalists described below travelled along established routes of exchange, including those of the YWCA and YMCA, and thus along the 'imperial fault lines' of Christianity that have long revealed the unevenness of British imperial rule.[6] Meanwhile, Indian liberal nationalists influenced by the internationalist agenda of the Theosophical Movement were, by the interwar decades, writing in a similar vein as Gandhi about India's rightful place as a moral force within the British empire.[7] As argued below, Australian theosophist Bessie Rischbieth shared this vision.

The opening section of this chapter concerns the cosmopolitan lives of three internationalists who were deeply engaged in promoting that world-view in the Pacific. As progressive commentators and educators, in the 1920s and 1930s each was concerned to strengthen dialogue between

Australia and India. Indian Christian Kotanda Rao visited Australia in 1936 as a representative of The Servants of India, where he offered a critique of the White Australia policy. Bessie Rischbieth, an Australian member of the Pan-Pacific Women's Association, went to India in 1930 as a convert to theosophy and on return told Australian audiences about her experiences. The only Indian delegate to the IPR's 1929 conference, S.K. Datta, who participated as a member of the British delegation, visited Australia following the First World War as part of his leadership role in the Indian YMCA. These individuals sought to increase cross-cultural understanding despite widespread anger among Asian nations at this period about the White Australia policy,[8] and Indian nationalists' attacks on the treatment of Indians resident in South Africa and Australia.[9]

Kotanda Rao in Australia

In the midst of growing world debate about the future of his own country, in 1936 Kotanda Rao arrived in Australia having just attended a conference on colonial education in Honolulu connected with the Pan-Pacific movement. Convened by the New Zealand anthropologist and Hawaiian university professor, Felix Keesing, and by former South African and Yale academic, C.T. Loram, the 'Education in Pacific Countries' conference ran over two months in Hawaii to investigate the role of 'native' education in the modernisation of colonial rule.[10] While a leading member of The Servants of India Society, an ecumenical Christian for whom Christian ethics was the basis for the modernisation of the Indian masses, Rao was highly critical of what he saw as Eurocentric thinking at the conference. In a commentary called 'A Critique of Some Assumptions', he criticised the use of 'Western Civilization' as though it were a universal fact rather than a set of knowledges with its own history. Western education did not 'belong' to Western peoples, he advised, and the impacts of Western industrialisation were not limited to the developing world but were felt everywhere, whether in Britain or India. Rejecting the Western superiority such assumptions implied, Rao preferred to universalise a set of moral values that he argued in theosophical fashion were the common source of the world's different belief systems and religions: 'truth, love and charity'.[11]

Arriving in Brisbane later that year, Rao was already half way through a world tour on behalf of the Society to investigate the conditions of Indians in various countries including Australia. With a letter of introduction from Gandhi in hand, he told the Australian press that the conditions of Indians in Australia seemed to have improved since the visit nearly 15 years ago of V.S. Srinivasa Sastri, India's representative to the League of Nations. In 1922 Sastri had had a mixed reception when he toured Australia, New Zealand and Canada on behalf of the Government of India to investigate the conditions of Indian nationals. The *Truth* doubted his 'sophistry', while the *Queenslander* described him a 'fine speaker' and one of the best to visit the state. Rehearsing the cultural defence of White Australia, in its commentary the latter expressed support for immigration restriction on the grounds that large numbers of Indians with their 'mode of life different from ours' would 'become a danger to our social life and institutions'. However, it accepted Sastri's argument that Indians living in Australia should be treated like other British subjects.[12]

Rao had been Sastri's personal secretary when he was India's Agent to the Union of South Africa following World War 1. Like many others of his generation, Gandhi foremost among them, this South African experience profoundly influenced Rao's views concerning the conditions of Indians living in the Dominions, leading him to promote Indian nationalism while acknowledging the 'mutual imbrications of East and West'.[13] Already in 1918 while on a visit to Britain, Rao spoke at a British Dominion Women's Suffrage Union meeting about the right of India to become a full member of the British Commonwealth.[14] Given the India Act of 1919 gave Indians a degree of rights within the British empire, disseminating information about the conditions of Indians living in the diaspora was an important objective of Rao's mission in Australia. Nearly 20 years later, he was no doubt aware that labour conditions in India, and particularly the role of caste in creating an underclass of untouchables continued to provide British imperialists with an argument against self-rule. And so he reassured the Australian public that The Servants of India was doing its best to tackle the problem of caste.[15]

Rao's world trip was important to him in other ways. As he proudly informed contacts he had made at the Honolulu conference, he had met his future wife Mary Campbell, a white American woman, while she was attending a teachers' conference at the same time in Hawaii.[16] When the couple set up house in Bangalore, they recalled their meeting by naming their new home 'Aloha' and Rao dedicated his book *Foreign Friends of India's Freedom* (1973) to Mary.[17] Various forms of intimate relationship and collaborative partnership between white women and Indian men are a feature of many of the cosmopolitan lives discussed in this book.

Bessie Rischbieth in India

Western commentators often viewed the prospect of Indian independence through the lens of their attitudes towards Indian culture and way of life. Rischbieth found beauty where many of her contemporaries in the British world saw ugliness and cruelty. The idea of the East as a resource for global renewal shared among internationalists like Rischbieth involved in British world and Pacific internationalism stands in stark contrast to representations of India by Western humanitarians who considered Hindu culture and ways of life to be fundamentally backward. Most notoriously, in her book *Mother India* (1927), Katherine Mayo railed against Indian traditions which she considered characterised by the betrothal of girl children, the sati of widows, and cruelty to animals. Ironically, as Sinha points out, Indian nationalist opposition to Mayo's internationally successful and sensationalist book provided middle-class Indian women with an unprecedented public platform, and led many, including Hannah Sen, Dhanavanthi Rama Rau, and Cornelia Sorabji, to seek out international venues through which to promote the liberal nationalist cause. These women became regular participants in international organisations like the Dominion women's British Commonwealth League (BCL), founded in London in 1925 as a sub-group of the International Women's Suffrage Alliance.[18]

Bessie Rischbieth was also involved in the BCL[19] as well as in the Pan-Pacific Women's Association.[20] She was keen to work with representatives of 'the East' whom she considered to combine the best elements from their own civilization with those of Western modernity.[21] (Fig. 5.1)

As a theosophist, Rischbieth admired Indian culture and modern Indian women.[22] In 1930 she had attended the All India Women's Conference held in Madras under the auspices of the Irish theosophist Margaret Cousins. She appears in the photograph in this chapter alongside Cousins; Dorothy Jinarajadasa, the English wife of the Sri Lankan president of the Theosophical Society and a founder of the Women's Indian Association established by Annie Besant in 1917; and Sarojini Naidu, the Civil Disobedience activist also involved in the formation of the Women's Indian Association. The 'outspoken' Naidu, who in 1925 had acted as the first Indian woman president of the Indian National Congress and presided over the East Africa Indian Congress in 1929, gave a keynote at the India Women's Conference in London in 1930 where, according to Rischbieth, she 'made a revolutionary speech... that India *would* have her freedom'. The flyer for

Fig. 5.1 Group of Women, All India Women's Conference, Madras, 1930. Rischbieth Papers. Ms 2004/11/569. Permission of the National Library of Australia

the Women's Conference, with her handwritten note on the back,[23] is among Rischbieth's papers along with photographs of her visit in the same year to the Sabarmati Ashram established by Gandhi in 1915 where she was required to spend part of her day hand spinning.

In a public lecture delivered on her return to Australia, Rischbieth named Mahatma Gandhi, the poet Rabindranath Tagore, and the biological scientist Sir Jagadish Chandra Bose as three of the most important men in the world. She also appealed to her audience to remember that the 'British empire is not a White Empire... [and so] to the British people as to no other people of this age comes the call to liberate the ancient culture of many races... ' Indeed, in the case of India, the 'great struggle for self-determination' was already underway as the arising nation sought to 're-clothe itself in all its old traditional beauty'. A supporter of Dominion status for India, she added: 'May India ever remain within the British Empire – free and untrammelled – the greatest link between East and

West, thus saving the best of each for the future civilization'.[24] Although Rischbieth did not directly critique the White Australia policy, she called upon Australia to recognise the best in both British and Indian cultures in order to fulfil its destiny as a modern nation within the British Commonwealth.

Undoubtedly many Western women's desire to be of service to India was integral to their search for careers as fellow modernisers of empire.[25] But their aims to uplift the East also brought some to see their own countries through others' eyes: that is, as sources of tradition as well as of progress. Nor was the West without its failings. A shift in attitude can be discerned, for example, in the pages of *Jus Suffragi*, the International Women's Suffrage Alliance newspaper. In 1922, it reported on the Girl Guides and the YWCA seeking 'to serve the girlhood of the East' by training them in the virtues of Christian service.[26] A few years later, however, reporting on the second Pan Pacific Women's Conference held in 1930, it quoted Australian delegate Bessie Rischbieth's conclusion that at this conference in the Pan-Pacific women from the 'older countries' of Asia were very interested in 'our social and industrial problems'.[27] Concerns about problems in Western countries reflected the global impact of Wall Street Crash of the 1930s and ensuing mass unemployment that spread also to India.

S.K. Datta, British (Indian) Delegate to the IPR

The YWCA and YMCA in Asia provided a key site for collective agency between modern individuals interested in Christian ecumenical and secular collaboration. Indeed, it was through these networks that a delegate from India was selected for inclusion in the British delegation to the IPR in 1929. The American progressive Edward Carter, the leader of the YMCA in India during the first years of the century had written to Sir Frederick Whyte at the Royal Institute of International Affairs in London, just as the IPR was taking shape in 1925, to remind him, that even though India was not 'one of the countries bordering on the Pacific... the relations of India, Australia, New Zealand, Fiji and the Strait Settlement are essentially a problem of the Pacific'. He recommended the inclusion of Indians on British delegations, with perhaps one a moderate and the other a more radical supporter of self-rule.[28]

Several years later, an Indian delegate was finally selected. Surendra Kumar Datta, who joined the British delegation of 1929, had been the national secretary of the YMCAs of India, Burma and Ceylon for a number of years, the president of the All India Conference of Indian Christians held in 1925, and a member of the Indian (or Imperial) Legislative Assembly. His 1908 training manual for young leaders titled *The Desire of India* had emphasised the ignorance and poverty embedded within the caste system and set out a trenchant critique of what he saw as a lack of regard for human life in India which, in his view, could only be overcome by adopting a progressive Christian approach to improving the standard of living, life expectancy and education among the masses.[29] Reflecting his commitment to educational reform, in 1917 Datta had contributed to an advisory committee on 'the educational needs of the mass movement' in India for the National Missionary Council in India.[30] His educational writing included 'India and Race Relationships' for *The Young Men of India* in 1924,[31] and he had participated in the education-focussed International Missionary Council conferences at Lake Mohonk, New York, in 1921 and in Jerusalem in 1928.[32] According to the American John L. Mott, a leading figure in the YMCA and World Student Christian Federation, the latter conference promoted the role of Christianity in secular progress and the force for good of 'interdenominational cooperation' between the 'various lands and races'.[33] Christian education towards social change had been pivotal to the Jerusalem International Missionary Conference in 1928, on the basis that Christian 'faith' would unite progressively minded people otherwise divided by religious or cultural belief.[34]

Datta had visited Australia in 1923 to study the YMCA and Student Christian Movement in that country and 'their reaction to the Christianising of the countries of Asia'. When asked about Gandhi, who was currently in jail for his leadership of the non-cooperative movement, Datta acknowledged Gandhi's popularity but added that, as a representative of the YMCA of India, an organisation which had no political affiliation, he supported membership of the British Commonwealth as the best outcome for his people. Datta explained further that he was influenced in this position by the Round Table group in England that promoted a 'Federated Commonwealth of free peoples'. At this point in his life he expressed adherence to a moderate nationalist position: he asserted that the British Empire had been a 'force for peace, goodwill and concord in the world', while arguing that it would now be of the 'highest interest of India to win for herself a place in this Commonwealth of free nations'.[35] Datta was later to adopt an increasingly radical political position, participating along with Gandhi as a representative of the Indian National Congress on the

Minorities Committee at the Second Round Table on India at Chatham House in 1931.

By the time of the IPR conference in 1929, Datta was married to an Irish woman, Rena Carswell. Carswell was already known for her 'Christian work among girls' in India by the time they met and in 1920 she had been elected 'Chairman of the Student Departments' at the Seventh Quadrennial Conference of the YWCA of India, Burma and Ceylon held in Ranchi, India.[36] Rena Datta continued to be active as an educationalist after her marriage, running the boarding house at Forman Christian College in Lahore while her husband worked as headmaster of that, the first Anglo-vernacular educational institution in India. In 1937 Rena Datta attended the All-India Women's Conference in Nagpur, indicating her support for social reform through improving Indian women's health and family life.[37]

Modernity in the Machine Age: The IPR Kyoto Conference of 1929

Held in the salubrious surroundings of the multi-storey Kyoto Hotel, the IPR's 1929 conference which S.K. Datta attended as a delegate was opened by Merle Davis, the general secretary of the IPR and the director of the Department of Social and Industrial Research initiated at the International Missionary Council conference in Jerusalemin1928. Davis had 20 years of experience in the YMCA of Japan. In his address, he spoke of the critical importance of understanding the 'contrasts in race, philosophy, social institutions, government and religion' across the Pacific. By protecting this diversity, the best from the various civilizations would become available to the whole of humanity: '...in this variety of ideals and in the various ways of life...lies the hope of the Pacific future....'[38] Davis went on to commend the IPR as a forum in which 'divergent opinions' were exchanged in friendly fashion, thanks to the supposedly new understanding of the 'psychological contrast' between East and West.[39]

Given the Pan-Pacific movement was formed on the premise that some peoples in the world, including those of India, required international support to become independent as nations, national identity here stood for the kinds of democratic values, citizenship rights and interest in international cooperation that would save the world from another war. It was a step towards, rather than a contradiction of, the desired cosmopolitan worldview through which individuals, peoples and nations would secure peace and prosperity. Under this rubric, becoming modern members of a modern nation would require some changes in traditional ways of life. Labour relations figured as one of these changes. In their discussions, the liberal Christian progressives active within the Pan-Pacific movement contrasted the modern factory worker with the figure of the 'coolie' (the indentured Indian subject created by British imperial rule) and the rural peasant who suffered terrible poverty and an oppressive caste system. Those living under these conditions were considered to be facing the combined impacts of rapid industrialisation and the abiding impediments of tradition. According to the Simon Commission, reporting on India's progress to the British government in 1928, it was for these reasons among others India was not ready for self-rule, let alone independence.

The potent association in Western minds between India and unthinking and unfeeling 'coolies' who supposedly lacked the capacity for national, let alone international or cosmopolitan, understanding of the world around them led the once pro-British Gandhi to conclude that only independence from Britain would secure India's future. The resilience of this negative evaluation of Indians' capacity to become modern, even in supposedly progressive circles, was underlined in a letter by another famous Indian nationalist, Rabindranath Tagore, that was being circulated confidentially among members of the American IPR in the 1930s.[40] Tagore reflected on the claim of an unnamed correspondent that to adopt poverty was to follow Christ's example and thus better understand the 'natives' of India. He rejected this argument as an example of the 'inveterate habit of proselytism' typical of the 'Western mind', evoking not so much Christ but the 'coolie recruiter trying to bring coolies to his master's house'.[41]

At stake in the discussions at the IPR conference in 1929 was agreeing on the appropriate speed of modernisation for the so-called peasant classes. A range of associated issues was debated in two interrelated conference round-tables titled 'Machine Age and Traditional Cultures' and 'Industrialisation'. These were topics intimately connected to the Indian nationalist cause, given that modernisation so often stood for the capacity to achieve independence. Some Western delegates were highly critical of the negative impact of industrialisation. One of the Australian delegates, the social economist Persia Campbell, had published a book on *Chinese Coolie Labour* in 1923 which argued that reform in labour relations had to proceed slowly, because: 'A man is something more than a "living machine."'[42] Becoming a wage labourer could bring about its own set of injustices, as had been shown by the Industrial Revolution in nineteenth century Europe. Arnold Toynbee, Professor of

International History at the University of London and a British delegate at the 1929 IPR conference, argued that the Industrial Revolution had destroyed the peasant way of life without improving economic and social conditions.[43] In contrast, other Western delegates argued that, if correctly handled, the coming Machine Age might yet cure the ills of all humanity. James T. Shotwell, the American who led the roundtable sessions, lectured widely in these years on the benefits of a new 'machine age' or post-Industrial Revolution that would advance human civilization. In Shotwell's analysis, the obstacle was not so much contained within technology itself but within the paucity of human understanding. Educating the masses about how to fulfil the promise of mechanisation would be as important for world peace as would be creating peaceful relations between nations.[44] Whatever the analysis, agreement appeared unanimous that better understanding the process of change taking place in the East might well be crucial to the future of world peace. When New Zealander, J. B Condliffe, a member of the IPR, reported to the Student Christian Movement of New Zealand on the rise of the East in world affairs he warned that: 'No-one knows what the result of their awakening may be; but they are not likely now either to accept European domination or to follow European industrialism in slavish imitation'.[45]

In the Pan-Pacific context, debate about the shape of Asian modernity necessarily focussed on the conditions of factory workers in China, Japan, and (at the IPR conference in 1929) India. The official conference report that year articulated the tension between the cosmopolitan project of friendly exchange and a desire to control the direction of modernisation in Asia:

> Western scholars interested in the question of cultural contacts between East and West must get beyond the question of controlling the impact of Western forces upon the East, and begin to ask what it is in Oriental life that accounts for the measure of adaptation and synthesis already achieved.[46]

If Japan was the most modernised country in the East, then the newly formed nation of China was considered the least advanced. Industrial reform in China had occupied the career of Eleanor Hinder, an Australian delegate who contributed as an expert on Australian industrial affairs at the Industrial Round Table. Hinder agreed that industrialisation followed stages emanating from European history, and she promoted international standards in her analysis of working conditions in Asia. But Hinder was also persuaded through her work with women in China under the auspices of the YWCA that the pace of factory reform in modernising

Asia should reflect also the internal needs and conditions of each nation.[47] And nor had colonial rule acted as a positive factor enabling change. In 1925, she told the *Mercury Hobart* in Tasmania that: 'In many respects the conditions of workers [in China] are similar to conditions in England a hundred years ago'. Moreover, even though 'Western capital' had been the source of these conditions, no effort 'was made by those responsible' to improve them.[48] Often China, in the words of Sophie Loy-Wilson, was seen by Australians as both the 'past and future of Australia', providing a warning about the impact of globalisation upon all workers.[49]

Along with slow modernisation, Chinese and Japanese delegates sought to stress the problematic impact of industrialisation on both physical and psychological welfare of workers in their nations. A Chinese woman delegate, Miss Hsia, said that the conditions of Chinese women in factories were particularly bad: 'In the cotton industry they are standing 10 hours; [the] Government in Nanking is very attentive to this matter. But [the] difficulty is that we cannot carry out this improvement plan at once. If we do it will be harmful to employers as well as workers'.[50] The same conditions concerned F.L. Ho (China) who reported that the recent Shanghai Child Labour Commission had produced some improvement in conditions, but many women and children still worked as long as 12-hour days, but according to the speaker this figure should be understood in the context of the 'different conception of working hours in China from the West'.[51]

Strikingly, the implication of the Machine Age for women workers in Eastern countries was a matter of personal experience for several of her fellow speakers. According to a Japanese daily report, strong opinions were expressed by 'Miss Sophie Tsen, President of the I Fang College in Changsha... who delivered a tirade... against the machine age noting three evil effects: it destroys individuality, impairs mental brilliancy and despoils the conscience'.[52] In the *West China Missionary*, Rev Brace, of the YWCA of China, reported that Dr Wu, Lady Principal of Ginling College, Nanking, spoke of her personal experience as a 'factory hand' and of 'the ease with which self-expression is lost in the machine age'. She added that the 'whole mechanistic system is the handmaid to war'.[53]

The speed of economic change and its impact on quality of life of Indian workers was also important to Datta. Reflecting at the conference on rapidly growing industrialisation in India, he began – as he had in his book *The Desire of India* – by describing the unregulated 'plantation system' established under British rule. The 'first industry of modern type' had been the textile industry that followed, where '[l]abour legislations [was] enacted to protect labourers. That is, 1. Factory legislation, 2. Welfare legislation, 3. Legislation to help labourers to organise themselves'.[54] In response to Dame Lyttleton's (Britain) comment that the fundamental aim of any reform should be to completely ban child labour,[55] Datta echoed the concerns of participants from China that the application of reform would need to progress slowly as their families had no other source of income. And although 'according to the Factory Act' children worked restricted hours, they still lacked access to education and experienced poor life expectancy. Indeed, he stated baldly: '[m]ost Indians are dead at 25'. Moreover, gender relations and family life more broadly had to be taken into account. Hitherto, efforts to bring education to the masses had been overwhelmed by extreme poverty in his country. Ultimately, the provision of: '[e]ducation [would be of] no use unless the standard of living of [the] family is raised so that children can be supported'.[56] Cosmopolitanism, here understood in terms of access to education, relied in the first instance on the basic local, and ultimately national, conditions of survival. In this setting, the ideals of cultural internationalism took second place to more fundamental human rights such as food and life expectancy.

Conclusion

Rather than judging nationalist sentiment in terms of rejecting or accepting Dominion status, Partha Chatterjee states that all Indian nationalists, in one way or another, adapted European civilization for their own use.[57] In her account of Indian women who participated in European-dominated women's international networks, Mrinalini Sinha similarly argues that their critiques of European universalism expressed both the 'simultaneous indispensability and inadequacy of European concepts' and a desire to make them 'potentially universal'.[58] Arguably, Indians like Datta treated similarly the cosmopolitanism espoused by Pan-Pacific internationalism: wishing to make a eurocentric worldview into one that was more inclusive. Australian, British and American Pan-Pacific internationalists hoped that the spirituality and communalism they saw in 'the East' would help to rehumanise European modernity. But the limits of these aspirations can be heard in first-hand accounts contributed by Datta and others concerning the actual conditions of Indian (or Japanese and Chinese) factory workers and the contradictory implications of universal reforms designed to improve their conditions that might well increase poverty and social dislocation).

In his report for the *West China Missionary News* on the IPR conference in 1929, Rev A.J. Brace, General Secretary of the YMCA in China, began with a rhetorical question: 'Is there a chance through friendly negotiation between plain citizens to narrow the field of conflicts between nations and... [thus] prevent conflict?' In his view, this chance *had* been embraced at the round-table discussions initiated by James Shotwell, the professor of History at Columbia credited with drafting the Kellog Peace Pact through which the international agreement had rejected war. According to Brace, Shotwell had instructed the members of round tables at the IPR to remain critical of the contradictory effects of progress upon human existence. The challenge for the world community was 'whether we can in our progress improve the greatest art of all – namely the science of living'.[59] According to Shotwell's own press report for the conference, he declared that 'In a Friendly Spirit Many Vexing Problems Disappear'.[60] In resolutely declamatory terms, Shotwell reiterated the official line of the IPR that it provided a uniquely cosmopolitan location for the synthesis of progressive Christian and secular thought. Here, the aspirational cosmopolitanism discussed in this book was articulated in the language of liberal reform, if, as has been argued, less evenly in interpersonal terms. It was at the interpersonal, however, that the problem of universalism was brought into debate.

For the Western participants the experience of Pan-Pacific was often experienced in rather self-consciously cosmopolitan fashion. According to Hinder, writing for *The White Ribbon Signal*, the Pan-Pacific movement gave Australian women the chance to find 'themselves matched in mentality and achievement' by their counterparts from 'Oriental countries'. This experience was particularly important for Australians where (thanks to White Australia) the 'homogeneity of the population is of itself an insidious factor inducing the idea that what differs from us is inferior to us'.[61] Thus, cosmopolitanism enacted at international conferences brought for many such delegates a realisation that what was considered advanced became problematic when critiqued by fellow delegates from so-called less modern countries. Indeed, differences between delegates seemed to become heightened when it came to discussing the expectations of the workers and the conditions of the masses in each of their countries.

While Pan-Pacific internationalism was implicated in these very inequalities, for many 'Western' and 'Eastern' participants conferences offered the possibility of enjoying the cosmopolitan experience of alternative 'zones of conversation' that seemed at least partially to exceed the parameters of empire.[62] While Datta's experience of the IPR or indeed Rao's impressions of Australia cannot be assumed, their interactions with Pan-Pacific cosmopolitanism seem unlikely to have made the same impact upon them as described by Hinder, Rischbieth and others. Indian nationalists educated in Christian mission or progressive networks were undoubtedly well versed in Australian, British and American ways of being cosmopolitan advocates of the British Commonwealth. And yet doubt can be heard at the end of the first session of the Industrialisation Roundtable, when Datta returned to the underlying question about the impact of factory work upon the individual, asking: 'Is there not a psychological feeling of suffering in being tied to a machine?'[63] His final question points to the ways in which the capacity of the non-Western subject to become modern and ultimately cosmopolitan was widely considered to be limited, especially the factory worker torn so recently from peasant life.

Whatever his thoughts on the success or otherwise of the IPR, Datta remained an enthusiastic supporter of the fostering international relationships between India, the USA, Britain and China. At the invitation of Edward Carter, he would attend as an observer for India at the IPR conference held in Mont Tremblant, Canada, in 1942, shortly before his death. He and Carter had remained close friends.[64] Indian representatives would also be among participants at the important IPR conference held in Hot Springs, a precursor to the formation of the United Nations in 1945.[65] While Carter who had been involved in the formation of an Indian Institute of International Affairs in 1935, an affiliate of the Royal Institute in London at Chatham House, during the increasingly anti-imperial rhetoric of the war years contributed to the establishment of the Indian Council of World Affairs through which Jawaharlal Nehru would convene the first Asian Relations Conference in 1947.[66]

Notes

1. Madeleine Herren, Martin Ruesch and Christiane Sibille, *Transcultural History: Theories, Methods, Sources* (Springer, Heidelberg, 2012): Part I.
2. Tomoko Akami, *Internationalizing the Pacific: The United States, Japan and the Institute of Pacific Relations in War and Peace, 1919–45* (Routledge, London, 2002): 85–86; C.A. Bayly, *Recovering Liberties: Indian Thought in the Age of Liberalism and Empire* (Cambridge University Press, Cambridge, 2011): ch 9.

3. Ritu Birla, 'Capitalist Subjects in Transition', in Dipesh Chakrabarty et al. (eds), *From the Colonial to the Postcolonial: India and Pakistan in Transition* (Oxford University Press, Oxford, 2007): 252.
4. CA Bayly, 'The Ends of Liberalism and the Political Thought of Nehru's India', *Modern Intellectual History*, 12:3 (2015): 605–626.
5. Tamsin Pietch, *Empire of Scholars: Universities, Networks and the British Academic World 1850 to 1939* (Manchester University Press, 2013): 450. See also Clare Midgley,

   'Indian Feminist Pandita Ramabai and Transnational Liberal Religious Networks in the Nineteenth-Century World', in Midgley et al. (eds), *Women in Transnational History: Connecting the Local and the Global* (Routledge, London, 2016): 13–32.
6. Jeffrey Cox, *Imperial Fault Lines: Christianity and Colonial Power in India, 1818–1940* (Stanford University Press, Stanford, CA, 2002); on the British Left, see Stephen Howe, *Anticolonialism in British Politics: The Left and the End of Empire, 1918–1964* (Clarendon Press, Oxford, 1993).
7. Mark Ravinder Frost, 'In Search of Cosmopolitan Discourse: A Historical Journey Across the Indian Ocean from Singapore to South Africa, 1870–1920', in Pamila Gupta et al. (eds), *Eyes Across the Water: Navigating the Indian Ocean* (Unisa Press, Pretoria, 2010): 79–80.
8. Marilyn Lake, 'Chinese Warnings and White Men's Prophesies', in Kirsty Reid and Fiona Paisley (eds), *Critical Perspectives on Colonialism: Writing the Empire from Below* (Routledge, New York, 2014): 46–57.
9. Marilyn Lake and Henry Reynolds, *Drawing the Global Colour Line: White Men's Countries and the Question of Racial Equality* (Melbourne University Press, Melbourne, 2008): 186–187.
10. Julie McLeod and Fiona Paisley, 'The Modernization of Colonialism and the Educability of the "Native": Transpacific Knowledge Networks and Education in the Interwar Years', *History of Education Quarterly*, 56:3 (2016): 473–502.
11. 'A Critique of Some Assumptions', S. Kodanda Rao, The Servants of India. *Education in Pacific Countries*, 301–304; quotations on 303 and 304. Proceedings, Vol 2. Institute of Education Library, London. Emphasis in original.
12. 'Sastri's Sophistry', *Truth* 2 July 1922: 6; 'Mr Sastri's Visit', *Queenslander* 1 July 1922: 9.
13. Meg Samuelson, 'A Community of Letters on the Indian Ocean Rim: Friendship, Fraternity and (Af-filial) Love', *English in Africa* 35:1 (2008): 29. See also Alison Bashford, 'Immigration Restriction: Rethinking Period and Place from Settler Colonies to Postcolonial Nations', *Journal of Global History* 9 (2014): 26–48.

14. Woollacott, *To Try her Fortune in London: Australian Women, Colonialism, and Modernity* (Oxford University Press, 2001): 122–123.
15. 'Indians in Australia. Greatly Improved Status', *Courier-Mail*, 17 November 1936, 17; and 'Discriminations Against Indians Here and in W.A.: Visitor Investigating Position', *The Telegraph*, 17 November 1936, 11.
16. Felix Keesing to Rao, 8 March 1938. Folder 5, 'February 1938–June 1938'. Felix Keesing Papers. Special Collections. University of Hawaii, Manoa (hereafter UHM).
17. Samuelson, 'A Community of Letters': 305.
18. Mrinalini Sinha, 'Suffragism and Internationalism: The Enfranchisement of British and Indian Women Under an Imperial State', *The Indian Economic and Social History Review* 36:4 (1999): 461–484; and Sinha, *Specters of Mother India: The Global Restructuring of an Empire* (Duke University Press, Durham, 2006).
19. Fiona Paisley, *Loving Protection? Australian Feminism and Aboriginal Women's Rights, 1919–1939* (Melbourne University Press, Melbourne, 2000).
20. Paisley, *Glamour in the Pacific*.
21. On women missionaries in India at the 'cutting edge' of modernity, see Margaret Allen '"That's the Modern Girl": Missionary Women and Modernity in Kolkata, c.1907–c1940', *Itinerario* XXIV:3 (2010): 83–96.
22. Jill Roe, 'A Shadowy Figure? Bessie Rischbieth, Theosophic Feminist', *Australian Cultural History* 23 (2004): 79–95; and Roe, *Beyond Belief: Theosophy in Australia 1879–1939* (New South Wales University Press, c1986). See also Frank Bongiorno, 'In this World and the Next: Modernity and Unorthodox Religion in Australia, 1880–1930', *Australian Cultural History* 25 (2006): 179–207. And see Kumari Jayawardena, *The White Woman's Other Burden: Western Women and South Asia during British Rule* (Routledge, London, 1995). See also, Alison Mackinnon, 'Knowledge Beyond Reason: Highly Educated Women and the Continuing Quest for Commensurability', *Australian Cultural History* 23 (2004): 59–78; and Angela Woollacott, 'From Moral to Professional Authority: Secularism, Social Work and Middle-Class Women's Self-Construction in World War 1 Britain', *Journal of Women's History* 10 (1998): 85–111.
23. 'India Women's Conference'. Printed Flyer. MS 2004/11/562, Rischbieth Papers, National Library of Australia (hereafter BRP).
24. 'Mahatma Gandhi: A World Figure', dated 1930. Hand written notes, several pages. Ms 2004/11/572, BRP.
25. Antoinette Burton, Dwelling in the Archive: Women Writing House, Home and History in Late Colonial India (Oxford University Press, Oxford, 2003);Catherine Candy, 'Competing Transnational Representations of the 1930s Indian Franchise Question', in Ian Christopher et al. (eds), *Women's*

Suffrage in the British Empire: Citizenship, Nation, and Race (Routledge, London, 2000): 191–206; Leila Rupp, *Worlds of Women: The Making of an International Women's Movement*(Princeton University Press, Princeton, 1997); Angela Woollacott, 'Australian Women's Metropolitan Activism: From Suffrage, to Imperial Vanguard, to Commonwealth Feminism', in Fletcher et al. (eds), *Women's Suffrage in the British Empire*, 207–223; Woollacott, *To Try Her Fortune*, 122ff; and Marie Sandell, *The Rise of Women's Transnational Activism: Identity and Sisterhood Between the World Wars* (IB Tauris, London, 2015): Chapter 7.

26. *Jus Suffragi* 16:10 July 1922, Supplement, p.1.
27. *Jus Suffragi*, 23:2 November, 18, and 23:3 December, 36. It would not be until 1952, however, that the All-India Women's Association sent a delegate to the PPWA. See Paisley, *Glamour in the Pacific*, 76 ff.
28. E.C. Carter to Frederick Whyte, 2 March 1927. E.C. Carter File, 6/4/12. Royal Institute of International Affairs Papers. Chatham House, London. Carter would lead the IPR into controversial waters in the 1930s and was later denounced as a radical. See Alan Roucher, 'The First Foreign Think Tanks', *American Quarterly* 30:4 (1978): 499.
29. SKDatta, *The Desire of India* (Church Missionary Society, London, 1908).
30. William Richey Hogg, *Ecumenical Foundations: A History of the International Missionary Council and its Nineteenth-Century Background* (Harper & Brothers, Publishers, New York, 1952): 177.
31. Margaret Allen, '"A Fine Type of Hindoo" Meets "the Australian type": British Indians in Australia and Diverse Masculinities', in Desley Deacon et al. (eds), *Transnational Ties: Australian Lives in the World* (ANU E Press, Canberra, 2008): fn 22.
32. Hogg, *Ecumenical Foundations*, 245.
33. John L. Mott, 'At Edinburgh, Jerusalem, and Madras', *International Review of Missions* 27:3 (1938): 304.
34. Jack Priestley, 'A New ERA – Beginning from Jerusalem? Some Reflections from 1928 on Matters Pertaining to 1988', *British Journal of Religious Education* 13:3 (1991): 143–151; and Peter Kallaway, 'Education, Health and Social Welfare in the Late Colonial Context: The International Missionary Council and Educational Transition in the Interwar Years with Specific Reference to Colonial Africa', *History of Education*, 38:2 (2009): 217–246.
35. 'Dr Datta's Position', *West Australian* Saturday 2 June, 1923, p. 8.
36. 'The YWCA', *The Pioneer Mail*, 31 December 1920, p. 35.
37. 'All India Women's Conference Sessions', Folder 11A 9668. United Nations Archives, Geneva.
38. 'Address by Merle Davis at the Opening Session', 5. B-3/6 Conferences – Kyoto 1929 – Proceedings #6. IPR Papers, UHM.
39. 'Address by Merle Davis', 6. Ibid.

40. Circulated by Dr G. A. Johnston Ross, an ecumenical preacher at Vassar in the United States. Ross preached Christianity as a social force in real life. See 'Sermon by the Reverend G.A. Johnston Ross', *The Vassar Miscellany News* IV: 47, 24 April 1920: 7.
41. 'A letter from Rabindranath Tagore. For private circulation only. (By courtesy of Dr. G. A. Johnston Ross) Institute of Pacific Relations Second Session – 1927', typed sheet, no date. IPR B-2/1, Conferences – Honolulu 1927 – Proceedings #7. UHM.
42. Campbell, *Chinese Coolie Emigration to Countries Within the British Empire* (P.S. King and Son Ltd., London, 1923): xvii.
43. David Cannadine, 'The Present and the Past in the English Industrial Revolution 1880–1980', *Past and Present* 103 (1984): 131–172.
44. Waqar Zaidi, 'Liberal Internationalist Approaches to Science and Technology in Interwar Britain and the United States', in Daniel Laqua (ed), *Internationalism Reconfigured: Transnational Ideas and Movements Between the World Wars* (I.B. Tauris, London, 2011): 22–24.
45. J.B.Condliffe, *The Third Mediterranean in History: An Introduction to Pacific Problems* with an introduction by John R. Mott (Student Christian Movement, New Zealand, 1926): 11.
46. 'The Third Biennial Conference of the Institute of Pacific Relations, Kyoto, Japan', 12. IPR B-3/1, Conferences – Kyoto 1929 – Proceedings #1, IPR Papers. UHM.
47. Sarah Paddle, '"For the China of the Future": Western Feminists, Colonisation and International Citizenship in China in the Interwar Years', *Australian Feminist Studies* 16:6 (2001): 325–341; and Paddle, 'The Limits of Sympathy: International Feminists and the Chinese "slave girl" Campaigns of the 1920s and 1930s', *Journal of Colonialism and Colonial History* 4:3 (2003): 1–28.
48. 'Oriental Industry. Welfare Work in China. Interesting Address by Miss Hinder', *The Maitland Daily Mercury* (Newcastle), 28 March 1925: 6.
49. Loy-Wilson, '"Liberating" Asia', 96.
50. 'Industrialization Report', 30 and 31 October 1929, 2. B-3/10 Conferences-Kyoto1929 – Proceedings #10, IPR Papers. UHM.
51. 'Industrialization Report', 31 October 1929, CHECK. B-3/10 Conferences-Kyoto1929 – Proceedings #10, IPR Papers. UHM.
52. Rev A.J. Brace, 'An Adventure in Friendship', *The West China Missionary News*, n.d., 33. Press clipping. B-4/8 – Kyoto Articles/Press Releases #2. IPR Papers. UHM.
53. Ibid, 33 and 34.
54. 'Industrialization Report', 30 and 31 October 1929, 2–3. B-3/10 Conferences-Kyoto1929 – Proceedings #10, IPR Papers. UHM.

55. 'Industrialization Report', 30 and 31October 1929, 3. B-3/10 Conferences-Kyoto1929 – Proceedings #10, IPR Papers. UHM.
56. 'Industrialization Report', 30 and 31October 1929, 3–4. B-3/10 Conferences-Kyoto1929 – Proceedings #10, IPR Papers. UHM.
57. Partha Chatterjee, 'Whose Imagined Community?', in Gopal Balakrishnan (ed), *Mapping the Nation* (Verso, London, 1996): 214–255.
58. Sinha, *Mother India*, 15–16.
59. Brace, 'An Adventure in Friendship'. IPR Papers. UHM.
60. Dr James T. Shotwell, 'When East meets West', Press clipping. B-4/8 – Kyoto Articles/Press Releases #2. IPR Papers. UHM.
61. Eleanor Hinder, 'Women in the Pacific', *The White Ribbon Signal*, 8 August 1929, 119.
62. Kris Manjapra, 'Introduction', in Sugata Bose and Kris Manjapra (eds), *Cosmopolitan Thought Zones: South Asia and the Global Circulation of Ideas* (Palgrave Macmillan, New York, 2010): 6.
63. 'Industrialization Report', 31 October 1929, 7. B-3/10 Conferences-Kyoto1929 – Proceedings #10, IPR Papers. UHM.
64. Anderson, 'Pacific Dreams', 74–75.
65. Tomoko, *Internationalising the Pacific*, 272–273.
66. Anderson, 'Pacific Dreams': 70.

CHAPTER 6

The Limits of Cosmopolitanism on the Cusp of Empire

Abstract The lives, friendships and encounters charted in this book reveal partial, uneven and contradictory processes at work in individual lives and across political and social movements. Engaging with knowledge and culture from around the globe at the same time as mediating its impacts through the spiritual and ethical consciousness that emerged out of everyday life was both a practical and a utopian pursuit. It was undertaken, as we have argued, in ways that were not straightforwardly derivative of Europe but which called into question the West's claims to provide a universal template of rights and conditions that was beneficial and applicable to the world as a whole.

Keywords Alternative cosmopolitanisms · Imperialism · Nationalism · Imperial networks · Global networks · Race · Transnational histories · Colorful cosmopolitanisms

We began this book with W. E. B. Du Bois' perceptive comment about 'the color line' as the key problem of the twentieth century. The cosmopolitan thought zones charted in this book appear to breach that 'color line' in the lives, friendships and encounters each of the case studies chart. Taken together, they reveal a range of alternative cosmopolitanisms that accommodated forms of amity, cooperation and confraternity in anti-colonial moves to end or ameliorate imperial relations of ruling.

J. Haggis et al., *Cosmopolitan Lives on the Cusp of Empire*,
DOI 10.1007/978-3-319-52748-2_6

However, the biographical approach we have utilised reveals partial, uneven and contradictory processes at work in individual lives and across political and social movements. This cautions us against constructing any simple trajectory from imperial to post-imperial, from racialised to anti-racist, or from colonial to anti-colonial. Nevertheless, we continue to believe in the importance of uncovering 'the mediated and bridged communities of affiliation that connected individuals and groups across lines of difference'.[1] Here, we consider the dynamics and limits of the alternative cosmopolitanisms embedded in our case studies, both individually and together, and we explore their implications for transnational histories of empire and its end, as well as for the study of globalisation and the cosmopolitanisms produced in its seams.

The cosmopolitanisms we have investigated emerged over the period 1860–1950, a period framed in the context of emergent anti-colonial nationalisms. Our case studies confirm Sugata Bose's argument that 'colorful cosmopolitans' are not constrained by the opposition of the national to the universal;[2] indeed, our examples suggest that it was not only 'colourful' cosmopolitans that could explore trajectories through the nationalist/universalist opposition. In Chapter 2, the sedentary Collet's ability to imagine India as her home in a way which convinced her Indian friends is suggestive of how re-positioning her original sense of national belonging was intrinsic to her cosmopolitanism. Polak's life-long activism on behalf of Indians and other subjugated individuals in the British Empire is discussed in Chapter 3 in terms of his ability to combine into a cosmopolitan activism his sense of being English, Jewish, Theosophist and at home in the world beyond nation and faith. In Chapter 4, a contrapuntal reading of Sykes and Patel's ethico-political journeys into cosmopolitan thought-zones and friendship reveals two very different pathways to a universal sensibility through negotiating the coloniser/colonised binary to arrive at a meeting point of amity and cooperation. The Pan-Pacific networks of the Institute for Pacific Relations, discussed in Chapter 5, show how even when actors are positioned as national representatives within internationalist spaces they articulate and strive for cosmopolitan global imaginaries of peaceful co-existence.

Alongside the shifting imperialism/nationalism dynamic, a key context for the cosmopolitan engagements of the individuals discussed in this book was the changing nature of religious and spiritual engagement across the borders of faith, and within imperial Christianity. The Brahmo Samaj trod an, at times, unsteady path between collaboration with westerners to promote social reform and assertion of a national identity traced through Hindu custom, as the furore over Keshub Chunder Sen's marriage attests. The emphasis on conversion by evangelical mission Christianity, tightly entwined with the imperial 'civilizing mission', produced unanticipated outcomes. 'Native churches', intended as spearheads of the twin mission to civilise and evangelise, increasingly articulated a decidedly independent cast of mind. At the World Missionary Conference in Edinburgh in 1910, Indian and Chinese Christian leaders lectured their mainly European audience on race as the problem bedevilling the Church. This was a turning point in imperial Christianity, signalling for some at least, the inevitability of building an ecumenical and inclusive international community of faith. In the Indian context, both the nationalist and ecumenical turn were inherited by the likes of S. K. Datta and Kotanda Rao, discussed in Chapter 5, and enabled them to combine a strong sense of nationalism with a powerful universalism of faith and politics embedded in discourses of anti-racism, social and economic justice. Christianity did not prevent Marjorie Sykes from building a shared cosmopolitanism embedded in the particularisms of Indian rural life, with Indian followers of Gandhi. For others, Theosophy melded east and west in ways that facilitated their cosmopolitanisms, as the examples of the British and Jewish intellectual Henry Polak, and the Australian feminist Pan-Pacific activist Bessie Rischbieth demonstrate.

As we have shown, liberal thinkers, activists and internationalists on both sides of colonial contact developed both informal voluntary networks of association (as discussed in Chapter 2 for example) and formal international organisations (as discussed in Chapter 5). These offered alternative spaces for respectful mutual interchange between Westerners and non-Westerners, which contrasted with official British-led imperial and colonial networks and were more conducive to the creation of a sense of cross-cultural affective community than the new Internationalist organisations such as the League of Nations and, later, the United Nations. These networks encouraged their members to question the subjectivities, structures and privileges of empire. In forming intimate, respectful and admiring relationships across the colour line, and taking on supportive rather than leadership roles in relation to colonial others, people like Collet, Sykes and Polak challenged the racist imperial worldview of colonised peoples as racially and culturally inferior, or at the very least as not-yet sufficiently modern to attain the conditions of individual or collective self-rule.

As this book suggests, it was often people who were in some way outside the religio-cultural mainstream that took the lead in forging cosmopolitan connections across the coloniser/colonised binary to address such issues. As well as the direct motor of cosmopolitan agency, faith can be understood as its biographical context. Polak's Jewishness, for example, can be seen as a cultural, historical and familial context that shaped his sense of marginality. Collet was part of a network linking heterodox Unitarians, considered heretics by some mainstream Christians, to Brahmos, many of whom had been ostracised by their Hindu families for breaking with caste prescriptions. Patel, from a Zoroastrian Parsee family, was positioned as a member of an ethnic and religious minority in India who were closely identified with the Raj. Sykes's decision to become a Quaker when working in India moved her Christian positioning from the nonconformist mainstream associated with the evangelical missionary movement to a dissenting group less concerned with religious dogma and Biblical authority, perhaps providing her with a cosmopolitan bridge to Gandhi's advocacy of non-violence as a Hindu spiritual practice. Rischbieth was a follower of theosophy who admired Indian civilization.

More broadly, colonised men and women challenging both indigenous social and religious norms and colonial racism and imperial rule found common ground with people like Collet, Sykes, Polak and Rischbieth. By reaching across narratives of difference embedded within the authority of imperial rule, however uneven or contradictory their standpoints on matters of race, economic inequality, or gender, the cosmopolitans considered in this book can be said to have mobilised affective forms of anti-colonial agency. They navigated 'race' and forms of religious or faith-based difference in the very decades in which the global colour line was being redrawn.

The Wider World of Imperial and Global Networks

The mainly liberal, middle-class, spiritually cosmopolitan women and men who feature in this book were also connected in various ways with the much broader world of cross-cultural interchange and movement connecting different parts of the world over the 1860–1950 period. As we stated in Chapter 1, the people we bring to the forefront in this volume were neither particularly famous nor subaltern. In this sense, we are recovering a middle ground between the elite who often dominated the formal sphere of Internationalism in this era, and the many millions who, through the disruptions thrust upon them by imperial globalisation, found cosmopolitan solidarities beyond their village, town or kin networks. In addition, we have focussed here on connections between white Westerners and Indians formed largely within the geopolitical framework of the British Empire. There is further work to be done on how these networks intermeshed with, operated alongside, and came into tension with developing Pan-Asian and Pan-African networks extending beyond the British imperial and broader Anglophone world, and the transnational solidarities forged between African-American activists and Indian nationalists.[3] The existence of an even more complex web of cross-cutting networks is hinted at by John Maynard's recovery of the influence of the African-American liberation movement led by Marcus Garvey on the beginnings of organised Aboriginal activism in Australia in the 1920s.[4]

In the case of our actors, a reaching out beyond empire-based networks came mainly through the faith-lines of liberal Christianity. The international contacts that S. K. Datta forged through his leading role in the YMCA in India, for example, opened up an opportunity to attend the IPR conference in Japan in 1929, and he was able to devise a route to his destination that took him through Southeast Asian ports, where he made contact with other anti-colonial liberals. His wife, Rena Datta, also forged close working relations through progressive Christian networks with African Americans and others working in South Africa for African civil rights.[5] In 1930, as Administrative Secretary at the World's Student Christian Federation, Geneva, she subscribed to 'Crisis', W.E.B. Du Bois' journal.[6]

As Antoinette Burton has warned with reference to the history of relationships between Indian and African nationalists, we must avoid the temptation to sentimentalise the history of attempts to create solidarity and constructive collaboration between activists variously racialised as brown, black or white.[7] In each of our case studies, we have tried to tease out the limits of the alternative cosmopolitanisms we depict. In Chapter 4, the reasons for Collet's apparently uncritical acceptance of British imperial rule are discussed. In Chapter 3, Gandhi and Polak are shown to have both been slow to extend solidarity and cosmopolitan equity to Africans, who suffered even harsher restrictions on citizenship and more dehumanising treatment humanity than Indian bonded labour. Chapter 5 reveals the difficulties encountered by different cosmopolitan actors in de-linking modernity from Westernisation, presaging contestations over the global rubric of International Development discourse that began in the late 1940s and continue to this day.

In 1944, Lady B. (Dhanvanthi) Rama Rau, the head of the Calcutta-based Society for Promotion of Education and Culture, and an influential campaigner for Indian women's rights,[8] expressed the Society's concerns in the face of the imminent likelihood of Indian independence. She stated that 'only when the youth of India becomes "World-conscious" and is enriched and stimulated by the cross-current of world thought, will its mind develop the full colour of its own personality'.[9] Amplified here is the thread found in so much of this book – the belief in the necessity of a cosmopolitan world-view to guard against the narrow parochialisms that nationalisms can foster. The Society's hope was that freedom and national independence, once achieved, would provide a conduit for interpersonal, international and global exchange and bring the 'best in Western and Eastern Civilization'.

Rama Rau's fears over Indian independence point to the larger questions that have been raised throughout this book about precisely what cosmopolitanisms, whether European presumptions of a singular universal, 'colored cosmopolitanisms', vernacular, alternative or aspirational actually mean. Tensions between the universal and the particular, the national and the transnational, and sameness and difference were inescapable features of the predominantly liberal cosmopolitan lives we have discussed in this book. In these circumstances, cosmopolitanism was indeed both aspirational and affective, expressed in the desire to engage with one's own inner hopes and dreams while also engaging with those of others. In acting on these desires, the individuals and networks studied here brought inner and outer worlds of possibility into greater alignment, acting as agents for change at both the local and the global level. Engaging with knowledge and culture from around the globe at the same time as mediating its impacts through the spiritual and ethical consciousness that emerged out of everyday life was both a practical and a utopian pursuit. It was undertaken, as we have argued, in ways that were not straightforwardly derivative of Europe but which called into question the west's claims to provide a universal template of rights and conditions that was beneficial and applicable to the world as a whole.

Notes

1. Kris Manjapra, 'Introduction' in *Cosmopolitan Thought Zones: South Asia and the Global Circulation of Ideas* ed. Sugata Bose, Kris Manjapra (Basingstoke, New York: Palgrave Macmillan, 2010), 15.
2. Sugata Bose, 'Different Universalisms, Colorful Cosmopolitanisms: The Global Imagination of the Colonized' in *Cosmopolitan Thought Zones*, 98.

3. Nico Slate, *Colored Cosmopolitanism. The Shared Struggle for Freedom in the United States and India* (Cambridge, MA, London: Harvard University Press, 2012).
4. John Maynard, *Fight for Liberty and Freedom: The Origins of Australian Aboriginal Activism* (Canberra: Aboriginal Studies Press, 2007).
5. David Henry Anthony III, *Max Yergan: Race Man, Internationalist, Cold Warrior* (New York University Press, 2006), 115–118, 124–127.
6. Student World, *Postcard from Student World to Crisis*, 31 January 1930. W. E. B. Du Bois Papers (MS 312). Special Collections and University Archives, University of Massachusetts Amherst Libraries.
7. Antoinette Burton, *Brown Over Black. Race and the Politics of Postcolonial Citation* (Gurgaon: Three Essays Collective, 2012).
8. Mrinalini Sinha, *Specters of Mother India: The Global Restructuring of an Empire* (Durham, NC: Duke University Press 2007), 167, 189, 191, 224.
9. 'Copy: The Society for the Promotion of Education and Culture. The Students of India', Elkin Papers Series 32, Box 150, 'India-Australia Association', File 11/1, The University of Sydney Archives.

Index

J. Haggis et al., *Cosmopolitan Lives on the Cusp of Empire*,
DOI 10.1007/978-3-319-52748-2

CPSIA information can be obtained
at www.ICGtesting.com
Printed in the USA
BVOW06*1501160617
5653BVAU00002B/2/P

9 783319 527475